A Walk Round Plugstreet

South Ypres Sector 1914 - 1918

Revised Edition

Mystic Plugstreet in the sunset glow
walk these gentle glades to know
that voices from yesteryear will call,
with a message soft as the leaves that fall.
Along Hunter Avenue like a silver thread,
past the cloistered elegance of the noble dead.

Tony Spagnoly

A Walk Round Plugstreet

South Ypres Sector 1914 - 1918

by
Tony Spagnoly
and
Ted Smith

with an introduction by
Jonathan Nicholls

Revised Edition

LEO COOPER

By the same group of authors in the Cameos of the Western Front series:

The Anatomy of a Raid
Australians at Celtic Wood, October 9th, 1917

Salient Points One
Ypres Sector 1914 - 1918

Salient Points Two
Ypres Sector 1914 - 1918

Salient Points Three
Ypres Sector 1914 - 1918

Poets & Pals of Picardy
A Weekend on the Somme with Mary Ellen Freeman

A Haven in Hell
Ypres Sector 1914 - 1918

In the Shadow of Hell
Ypres Sector 1914 - 1918

First published 1997
Revised edition published 2003 by
Leo Cooper/an imprint of Pen & Sword Books Limited
47 Church Street
Barnsley
South Yorkshire S70 2AS

Front cover design by Ted Smith from an idea by Jim Ludden

A CIP catalogue record for this book is available
from the British Library
ISBN 0 85052 570 5

Typeset by IMCC Ltd. in 9.5 point Garamond
Printed in Great Britain by
CPI UK

CONTENTS

This book is dedicated to the memory of
Rifleman Albert E. French,
18th Battalion King's Royal Rifle Corps,
who was killed in action at
Ploegsteert Wood on 15 April, 1916.
He was 16 years old when he died and he lies in
Hyde Park Corner (Royal Berks) Cemetery, Ploegsteert.

The Kid

Come on kid beneath your mound
What are you doing there?
So quiet, so still ... alone in your tomb
I can only stand and stare.

I could have passed on by ... perhaps I should
For my mood is pretty sad
To know you are there, cut down in your prime
In a world gone truly mad.

I try so hard to picture your face
And to figure what did it mean?
But it always comes back to you again
And a sense of what might have been.

I ponder the end as it comes to you
As the evening light now fades
I feel an awful sense of anger
At the terrible price you paid.

Stillness lies all around me
I see your friends surround your grave
Their tears mingle with earthly dust
For all you had ... you gave.

I know they greatly loved you
Now they have joined you each in turn
So much loss ... and Oh, such sadness
Are there no lessons we can learn?

The night hawks circle above you
There is nothing they have not seen
Me Kid? ... well I'm desolate when I touch your stone
For you were only sixteen.

Tony Spagnoly

Acknowledgments

Most of the new information and photographs in this edition have been gathered with the cooperation of the people of Ploegsteert. Particular appreciation is given to Claude and Nellie Verhaeghe-Leleu, proprietors of L'Auberge restaurant directly opposite the Ploegsteert Memorial on the Messines Road whose computer, scanner, email facility, photographic archive, local knowledge and contacts and, equally as important, their coffee machine, proved indispensable; to Thierry Vantorre (for his help in obtaining information on The Catacombs); to Patrick Roelens (for permission to use his photographs of the concrete structures within the wood and the information he supplied on Private Harry Wilkinson, the remains of whom he found and reported to the local authorities) and, of course, to Marcel Leplat the 'Plugstreet Postcard King'.

Thanks go to Harry Canvin for liaising with the family of Rifleman Albert French, 18th Battalion King's Royal Rifle Corps, to whom this book is dedicated and to David Isaacs for his help with information on Rifleman Reuben Barnett, 1st Battalion Rifle Brigade. Others include Tom Gudmestad, U.S.A.; Paul Reed, France; Sue Brophy who composed the poem on Rifle House; Lawrence Farrow for supplying material on Ploegsteert; and John Woolsgrove and Christine De Deyne for the use of The Shell Hole in Ypres as a base

In recent years, there has been an explosion in the number of books and publications on every aspect of the Great War of 1914-1918. Most of them, like this one, would not have had a chance of lift-off without access to the national archives held by The Commonwealth War Graves Commission, The Imperial War Museum, The Public Record Office and The Australian War Memorial located in Canberra.

Thanks go to James Brazier for his work in proof-reading the original draft and to Corinne Smith for hours of typing and re-typing the text, and for her patience and fortitude in keeping three young children (now not so young) amused in a motorcar parked in the middle of nowhere while her husband walked about outside, seemingly staring at deserted roads and empty fields.

Gratitude goes to Major (Rtd) R.D. Cassidy MBE, Secretary of the Rifle Brigade Club and Association, for his permission to use photographs from The History of the Rifle Brigade in the War of 1914-1918; to Tonie and Valmai Holt of Battlefield Tours fame for permission to include Old Bill material; and to the late John Laffin who helped identify the site of the southerly openings to The Catacombs at Hill 63.

A full bibliography is listed at the end of this book and it is to those authors who have gone before us that we owe an unrepayable debt.

Ted Smith, July 2003

AUTHOR'S PREFACE
Tony Spagnoly

Plugstreet, another one of the many names of hamlets, villages and towns that dotted the Western Front owes its notoriety, not only to the events of that war, but to the British soldier's adaptation of its native spelling to something more suitable for his palate. Hence Ploegsteert became Plugstreet or Plug Street.

I can remember quite clearly when my interest in the place named Plugstreet Wood began to develop and grow. In 1964 the London Evening Standard newspaper, in its commemoration of the outbreak of the Great War in August 1914, commissioned Henry Williamson, already well known for his writings on nature and wild life, to write a series of articles covering his experiences on the Western Front. These experiences had a tremendous influence on Williamson and, in the post-war years when he settled down to lead his life close to the rugged north Devonshire coast, the places where he served in Flanders, Artois and Picardy became the centre point of his life's work. This resulted in him producing one of the most magnificent and popular works in English literature, A Chronicle of Ancient Sunlight, a semi-fictional story covering the main strands of his life in war and in peace.

I remember quite vividly one of the newspaper articles he entitled A Return to the Wood of Plugstreet. The photograph he used to illustrate it was a rather poignant one of the headstone of Rifleman Reuben Barnett of the 1st Battalion Rifle Brigade who had been killed in action on 19 December 1914. The Star of David on the stone denoted he was of the Jewish faith, and he was only 15 years old. I have never forgotten that picture or the sad message it conveyed. Rifleman Barnett must have been one of the youngest soldiers to lay in the wood, if not one of the youngest casualties in the whole of the Ypres Salient at that time. My mind began to work overtime wondering who he was, what had he looked like and how he had been killed. Had anyone ever visited his grave? Did friends and colleagues from Stoke Newington know of his fate? Had this young Jewish lad been unmourned all these years?

The 19 December 1914 had been a particularly traumatic day for the 1st Battalion Rifle Brigade as it had been, likewise, for the 1st Somersets and the 1st Hampshires, all of the 11th Brigade, 4th Division. They had moved forward from the eastern edge of the wood across the cloying mud of No-Man's Land to attack the strongly defended enemy strongpoint known as The Birdcage. The powers that be at that time had decided that pressure applied here in the Plugstreet sector would stop the enemy opposite being used as reserves in the south and thus ease the pressure that the French were under in Artois. In the event, the attack was an unmitigated failure causing over 250 casualties to the attackers, leaving the enemy wire unbreached.

Rifleman Barnett had been one of the casualties that lay before the German wire that sad dawn, just six days before the Christmas Truce when British and German met to converse, exchange gifts and generally celebrate the birth of the Prince of Peace. It was during this truce that it was agreed between the opposing forces that the British casualties of that disastrous raid of 19 December could be collected for burial. A military cemetery within the wood had been started close to the log hut used as the Rifle Brigade headquarters. This plot became known as Rifle House Cemetery and today is most certainly one of the more tranquil and pleasant resting places for British casualties on the Western Front. Two hundred and twenty-nine men found their last resting place here including many from that fateful attack of the 19th, Rifleman Barnett among them in Plot IV. E10. One can only wonder and surmise at the thoughts of the carrying party during its trek from The Birdcage to the small burial plot in the middle of the wood as to the youthful features of their pitiful load. Who ordains thus?

Many times since 1964 when I read that article I have visited Rifle House Cemetery and stood before this young warrior, hoping he knows that he is not forgotten. Each time, I have placed a pebble on his headstone, a Hebrew gesture of remembrance taught me by Jewish friends, to let those who follow know that someone has passed this way to visit.

Henry Williamson also left me with a deep understanding of his feelings which have captured for me the essential magic of this place when he summed up his experiences in the wood with the words: "All through the long years since the war when I smell burning charcoal, hear a wood-pigeon calling, or feel the crunch of hoar frost under my feet, time falls away, and I am back again in Plugstreet Wood". For some reason, these words have affected me profoundly and dramatically. His recollections and recall of the attack on The Birdcage dug deep, and so was born my fascination with this woodland on the southern tip of the Belgian sector of the old Western Front. This fascination has been deep and abiding and all the time and energy I have devoted in researching and just tramping this area has been well rewarded.

The wood was never a scene of any set-piece battle and nothing of real import occurred there, except for a brief period of infantry action in October 1914 and again in the summer of 1918 when it fell into the hands of the Germans during their advance on Mont Kemmel. The British 29th Division quickly remedied that situation in the September of that year.

For much of the war, both sides used the general area to instruct fledgling battalions into the lore and mysteries of life in the front line. Parts of the wood took on a thin skeletal appearance due to the sporadic shelling at tree-top level. It drew the full attention of the British artillery only once, that when Plugstreet was briefly inhabited by the German forces in 1918. Even after that onslaught it was never bereft of its full foliage, often the fate of wooded areas in the combat zone. This three-by-one-and-a-half kilometre plantation-type growth maintained the general appearance of its pre-war role, the main woodland in the Hennessy cognac family estate. The baronial château, Château de la Hutte, sited on the eastern slope of Rossignol Hill, better known to the troops as Hill 63, identifying its height in metres as shown on maps of the period, was destroyed by gunfire during the war and was never rebuilt. The ruins can still be seen on the skyline of the hill from the main Armentières-Messines road.

Many notables graced the wood with their presence during their military service. A study of these characters can well enhance the area of Ploegsteert for the military historian, researcher and everyday pilgrim. As well as Henry Williamson, they included:

Sir Winston Churchill, Prime Minister, 6th Royal Scots Fusiliers;

Sir Anthony Eden, Earl of Avon, Prime Minister, 21st King's Royal
    Rifle Corps;

Roland Leighton, poet, 7th Worcestershire Regiment;

Bruce Bairnsfather, illustrator, cartoonist and creator of 'Old Bill',
    1st Warwickshire Regiment;

Richard Barrett Talbot Kelly, artist, 9th Divisional Artillery;

Ronald Poulton Palmer, England rugby captain,
    1/4th Royal Berkshire Regiment.

Adolf Hitler serving at Messines in the winter of 1914, just prior to his being awarded the Iron Cross at Bois Quarante, Wytschaete, is worth a mention. Although he never trod the wood, he was near enough on a daily basis to have been aware of its brooding presence. It is strange to think that he and Churchill, the two men who conducted World War II, were serving in the same area, though not at the same time, in another war twenty-five years previously.

Many famous personalities and writers who served in the war have pronounced on places having had most impact on them but, for me, those articles written by Williamson in 1964 vibrate strongest down the years. "The smell of charcoal", "a wood-pigeon calling", "the crunch of hoar frost under my feet", these words, recalling the smells and sounds of Plugstreet, sum up exactly what the wood means to me today. To walk its quiet glades, to tread its gentle rides, seeing and appreciating the odd violet, as did Roland Leighton, is what Plugstreet Wood offers. To visit the quiet and isolated cemeteries and pay tribute to its thousand 'guardians' lying in and around it, and to give particular thought to Rifleman Reuben Barnett and Rifleman Albert French, provides a deep and satisfying reflection, with tranquil thoughts in silent solitude.

Rifleman Albert French was another young soldier whose tragic story had captured my attention. This lad from Wolverton, Buckinghamshire had only been in the sector for a few weeks in June 1916 when he was killed in action in the wood as he helped to sandbag the defences along the front of the 41st Division. A letter from the chaplain, Captain M. Mayne, states poignantly: "Four bullets from a machine gun hit him, and he died instantaneously. He lies buried amid brave comrades in a wood, and his grave is carefully tended by his friends in the battalion." Many visitors to his grave in the neat little burial enclosure of the Hyde Park Corner (Royal Berks) Cemetery, Ploegsteert, pay their respects to this young warrior, especially since a BBC radio programme based on his short life and his letters from the front was broadcast in the early 1970s.

This is the reward of Plugstreet Wood for the sensitive soul. Henry Williamson was right, the memories of the wood on a quiet summer's day stay with you forever. The atmosphere is like a magic balm and the spirit is eternal and abiding.

Hopefully this book, this battlefield companion, will not deprive you of the underlying calm and embracing serenity of Plugstreet Wood by outlining some of the more violent and dramatic events that happened in its vicinity during those turbulent years 1914 to 1918.

AUTHOR'S FOREWORD
Ted Smith

Ploegsteert, or Plugstreet, is the name of a small village in the commune of Comines-Warneton in West Flanders, Belgium, edging the French border close to Armentières. Apart from its industrious community and agricultural surrounds, its main features are a 63-metre hill - Rossignol Hill (Hill 63 to the British Army during the Great War) - and a wood - Bois de Ploegsteert or Bois de la Hutte to the Belgians and the French. Simplified to 'Plugstreet Wood' by British troops billeted in the area in 1914, it kept that title for the rest of the war. The commune is traversed by two rivers, the River Douve and the River Warnave, both tributaries of the River Lys, running respectively to the north and south of the wood. Throughout the war Ploegsteert was always in British hands, except for a time in 1918, and faced the enemy occupied territory – to the north on the heights of the southern slopes of the Messines Ridge and eastwards towards Warneton. Although never an embattled part of the Western Front in Belgium, much happened there, and it meant many different things to the multitude of regiments who billeted in this south Ypres sector at various times during the Great War.

The village of Ploegsteert itself is situated on the south-west corner of the wood and is typical of the many villages in this southern part of Belgium, with its church, village square, a number of estaminets and a main street. Troops were billeted in and around the village throughout the war, and it remained relatively undamaged until the German Offensive in 1918.

The main road from Armentières in France running northward to Messines, then onward to Ypres, bisects the village square and, on its way to Messines, slices through the western edge of the wood separating the hamlet of La Hutte and Hill 63 from the main body of the wood.

The road running due east from the village square crossroads leads to the hamlet of Le Gheer on the south-east corner of the wood. No more than a few houses, a café, a calvary at the crossroads and an hospice (a convent during the war years), it suffered from heavy shell-fire damage because of its proximity to the front-line between the British, who held it, and the Germans a few hundred yards eastwards across No-Man's Land.

The secondary road leading north out of Le Gheer virtually followed the front-line along the eastern edge of the wood, past the infamous

'Birdcage' to the even tinier hamlet of St. Yves, then a small grouping of shell-ruined cottages and buildings. A small road winds through the hamlet then turns to the west along a small ridge north of the wood meeting the main Armentières-Messines road at a widespread grouping of dwellings calling itself La Hutte, nestling on the eastern slope of Hill 63. This dominant height, overlooking the valley of the River Douve and opposite the even more dominant rise of the southern edge of the Messines Ridge was defended by lines of trenches and self-contained strongpoints, and was of great strategic importance to the British.

From 1914 to 1917, the Germans occupied the Messines Ridge, including the village of Messines with its distinctive church steeple visible to the British troops across the river below. Both combatants from their respective viewpoints would bring down artillery fire against the other whenever, and wherever, they felt so disposed. The gunfire-destroyed Château de la Hutte, sited on the eastern slope of Hill 63, was surrounded by gun batteries and its vast cellars were used as shelter by artillerymen and infantry alike. Many of the regiments serving in the area based their battalion headquarters in wooden shacks behind the hill and up the valley of the River Douve in concrete quarters under buildings such as La Plus Douve Farm and St. Quentin's Cabaret. The western and southern slopes of the hill, being well hidden from the prying eyes of enemy observers, were dotted with troop mustering points for all sorts of units supporting the infantry - rations, clothing, ammunition, special items (mainly gum-boot supplies for working parties on their way to Plugstreet Wood) and general store dumps. On the southern base of the hill, Rosenberg Château and Underhill Farm were used as troop billets and dressing stations with their respective burial plots close by. On either side of the main Armentières-Messines road, burial plots were started and cared for by the regiments billeted in Plugstreet further down the road.

This then is the area, within and without the wood, about which this book is entitled and written. It points to the places where men lived, fought and died during those years of 1914 to 1918, but it cannot recreate the smells, the shell-holed muddy paths, the filth, the shell-splintered trees, the noise, the ever present danger, the fear and anguish, the weariness, the tension, or the sorrow and grief for friends passed. All that is for the imagination and the perception of the reader.

INTRODUCTION

Once again I am privileged to write a short introduction to Tony Spagnoly and Ted Smith's third book. This time, on a part of the old Western Front close to their hearts and mine: Plugstreet as it was called by the Tommies. Alas, it is no longer a household name as it was to the fading generation who fought the Great War of 1914 - 18.

During the autumn of 1979, I took a few days' break from the busy Hampstead police station to visit the Ypres Salient with my wife, mum and dad (their fathers had both served on the Western Front), and infant son. Making an early morning start from our base in Armentières we arrived at Plugstreet Wood, driving down the track to Prowse Point. There, among inquisitive cattle, we left the car. The remainder of the journey was made on foot and I well remember the mud clinging to the wheels of Greg's pushchair as we walked along the quiet glades. The purpose of our visit was The 1st Buckinghamshire Battalion plot in Ploegsteert Wood Military Cemetery where lay young men from our neighbourhood back home. It was a first and most memorable visit. The brooding darkness of the tall trees and the dripping dampness of the rides were suddenly lifted as we entered the sunlit cemetery. Its stunning, silent beauty only interrupted by the calls of wood pigeons. The wood opened its wide arms to us. We were among friends.

That first visit to Plugstreet Wood led to many more and I have been there every year since, mainly, with a small coach party. Before each trip, it was my habit to pick up the telephone and 'tap' Tony Spagnoly for snippets of information about the wood. Each time he told me something new and, invariably, the following day a long handwritten letter, containing much fascinating detail, would drop through my letterbox. I now have enough of his letters to write my own book.

During those early days, however, I suspect I was regarded by my police colleagues as a First World War 'train spotter.' - even though I never wore a wax jacket, green wellingtons or an anorak of the associated kind. And, doubtless today, along with other fellow members of The Western Front Association who go on 'remembering' I am still regarded the same, and the name of Plugstreet among my contemporary pals who drink in the White Lion at Apsley is an alien word. "Is it from the Beano?" was one recent question.

Thankfully, Tony Spagnoly and Ted Smith have rectified matters in splendid fashion with this delightful little book which will, hopefully, restore the name of Plugstreet to the English language. More important, it will be indispensable to all intended pilgrims to Plugstreet Wood and its surrounding area. Read it before you go. It will reveal to all who carry the torch, more secret knowledge of another British corner of a foreign field.

I long to return to Plugstreet Wood, to feel the welcome embrace of its branches and to walk its cool glades. To, once again, follow in the footsteps of brave men and, perhaps, hear an echo of those familiar old songs whispering gently through the wind in the trees. In the words of Edmund Blunden:

"I must go over the ground again. A voice, perhaps not my own, answers within me. You will be going over the ground again, it says."

This little book will ensure that!

Jonathan Nicholls, 1997

EDITOR'S NOTE

This revised edition of the book features further information and detail of activities in and around Plugstreet and its wood which have come to light since the book's original publishing date of June 1997. Virtually all the new content was contributed by members of the local community and the extra photographs included in the book were either supplied by them, or taken using information and guidance from them.

The lie of the land in the Plugstreet sector of Belgium is such that the lower portion of the area, that part edging the border with France, is virtually at sea level, with the northern portion on slightly higher ground, Rossignol Hill (Hill 63), the St. Yves Ridge, (in the war years often referred to as St. Yves Hill), and the southern slopes of the Messines Ridge being its highest points. The River Lys and its multitude of small tributaries running in all directions from the main flow cause many places to form marshy, boggy ground which in the winter become totally waterlogged. Two of the larger tributaries are the River Douve and the River Warnave running north and south of the area respectively. In between these two rivers to the east of the area is Plugstreet Wood where the front line in the Great War ran from below the hamlet of Le Gheer, up along the wood's eastern fringe then swept westward over it to cross the Armentières-Messines road just south of a large farm, then a German strongpoint, called La Petite Douve Farm. The lower portion of the wood is in the sea level section of the area and the thought of digging anything in the vicinity, let alone trenches for human occupants, is out of the question - except in military thought.

This is the countryside where, in the early battles of 1914, men fought and died in water-filled ditches masquerading under the name of trenches. In those early days, battalions seldom took more than a few days' rest from the front because of the lack of reserves to replace them. Trench lines were just taking shape and lacked any form of comfort, with men being expected to stay in them in abominable weather conditions until relieved. Trenches were mere holes in the ground and communication between front and reserve lines was not considered to be of major importance, ammunition and supplies being scrambled across open ground by men who took such chores for granted - if they survived them. With no structured communication trenches, men could not move about during the daylight hours with movement between the support and front-line trenches being restricted to the night, and then crouching under showers of bullets and shells. Troops from both sides stood in trenches, often filled with water, for long periods without any form of movement to warm their freezing and wet bodies. The ground around the trenches would become battered and torn with shell holes which would fill with water, forming pools of slime. In these would fall the remains of bullet-ridden bodies of the fallen of both sides, adding to the already hideous stench of cordite and the smells of hundreds of unwashed human beings.

After 1914, the situation did 'improve', not only because individual, face-to-face action became a thing of the past but because the Royal Engineers became involved with strongpoint development in the front-line. Trench lines generally became more professional and sophisticated, designed with men, movement, safety and a degree of comfort in mind - the London Rifle Brigade built a stretch of reserve trenches and dugouts along the Armentières-Messines road between La Hutte and Plugstreet village that would have won design awards in another era.

The sector, although not falling silent, certainly became less active in 1915 and 1916 but, in 1914, nobody would have believed that: "Plugstreet was of great value for the safe assembly of troops. It was traversed by a network of wooden paths raised above ground level, for the wood becomes a marsh after heavy rain" and woe betide the man who would dare to have uttered such sentiments to the troops of the 4th Division who served there.

From 1915 until the war's end, static warfare had become the norm and the fighting demands on the infantry lessened, although this didn't affect the long hours of labour expected of them in the dark hours. Except in major battles, and as prisoners, the enemy was rarely seen and the artillery took on the mantle of the important arm, the gunners taking-out more than their fair share of aggression on the enemy, but taking heavy casualties in return.

After 1914, regiments did speak highly, if not fondly, of Plugstreet and, all in all, if war must be waged, then what nicer surroundings than in or near a large wood.

Ted Smith, July 2003

TRIBUTE

On 7 June 1999 a ceremony took place at the Ploegsteert Memorial inaugurating the sounding of *Last Post* at 7 pm on the first Friday of every month. Organised and implemented by the local community through the *Comité du Memorial de Ploegsteert*, the monthly ceremony was devised to show their gratitude to, and to honour the memory of, the many thousands of Allied troops who made the ultimate sacrifice during the Great War of 1914 – 1918

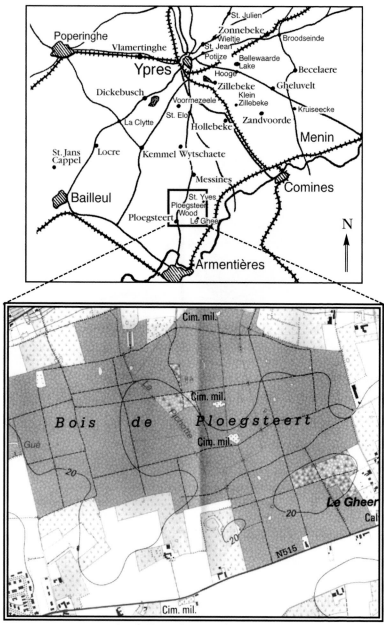

South Ypres Sector - Plugstreet

BEGINNINGS

The dismal rain was dripping from the peak of the Colonel's cap,
The waterproof sheets were streaming, but who of us cared a rap?
The dreary dark closed round us, but blithe we took the trail
And trudged the pave highway from Hazebrouck to Strazeele.

From Hazebrouck to Strazeele,
Le Bizet through Nieppe,
And on to Ploegsteert Village
Is only just a step;
Where the long battle-line
Curves round the battered wood,
We set our faces to the foe,
And made our promise good.

Short days of wintry weather, long nights of rain and cold,
We fought the slithering parapets and stalked the foeman bold;
We dug and drained and built a sector for a king -
And there were fewer of us when we marched out in the spring.
From Ploegsteert to La Creche
And back into Strazeele It isn't much I grant you
To spin in to a tale.
But now we have a story - It's bloody, but it's good -
And most we've done we learned to do In front of Ploegsteert Wood.

Lieutenant Colonel John Stewart
4th Battalion the South Staffordshire Regiment
Killed in Action 26 April 1918 Aged 28.
Tyne Cot Memorial to the Missing

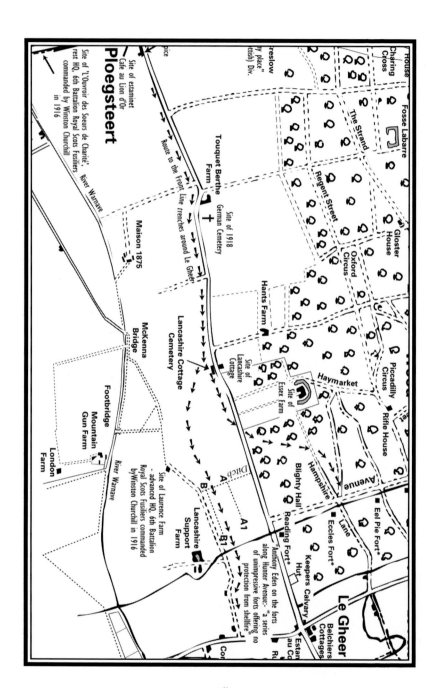

CHAPTER 1

PLUGSTREET TO LE GHEER

PLOEGSTEERT VILLAGE WITH ITS LITTLE SQUARE embracing the Mairie, a café, a few small stores and a church with its towering steeple dominating one corner of it, was battered during the war but never totally destroyed. German shells claimed their share of the church's brickwork in the first stages of the war in this part of Belgium, but the adjutant of the 6th Royal Scots Fusiliers noted in early 1916 when the regiment first arrived in the village that:

> The church tower, a very high one, still held its head aloft for the gratification of the superstitious.

Today, its churchyard houses the tiny Ploegsteert Churchyard British Military Cemetery with its nine headstones set in a single-line among the graves of the local community, and the Mairie alongside the church boasts a plaque on its

outer-wall commemorating Sir Winston Churchill's service in the area in 1916. The plaque was unveiled in 1991 by his grandson, Winston Churchill, Member of Parliament, during the ceremonies dedicating the sixtieth anniversary of the inauguration of the Ploegsteert Memorial to the Missing at Hyde Park Corner north of the square at the foot of Hill 63 on the road to Messines. Once facing each other on opposite corners of the crossroads in the village square were the two estaminets, Aux

The plaque on the Marie wall in Ploegsteert village commemorating Sir Winston Churchill's service in the area during 1916.

Trois Amis and Café au Lion d'Or, both much frequented by British troops enjoying what little leisure time they had between duties during their periods of service in the sector. Today only one of the buildings remains in place, now privately owned, it still displays the name Aux Trois Amis on its outer wall, but the occupants no longer sell 'pomme-frites', omelettes, cheap wine or beer. Café au Lion d'Or was demolished during the rebuilding of the crossroad area in 2003 and its site, no longer housing a building, is now just a patch of lawn on what was once a street corner.

Other than the foregoing, there is very little in the village or its square to remember the men of the many regiments who spent much of their free time here in private houses, and in and around the estaminets. The village billeted

troops from a multitude of different regiments in private homes, the schoolhouse, public buildings and outlying farm complexes, with a large brewery on the left-hand side of the road to Armentières acting as a major bathing facility for large numbers of men. The brewery was eventually razed to the ground by gunfire during the war and never rebuilt, domestic properties now taking its place on the corner. Another brewery in Nieppe was also used periodically for bath facilities where troops would rid themselves of the ever-

The village church in November 1915.

Winston Spencer Churchill grandson of the Right Hon Winston Churchill unveils the plaque commemorating his grandfather's service in the Ploegsteert sector in 1916.

present lice and be issued with fresh, clean kit – in which the lice would soon re-establish themselves until the next trip. Other hutted camps and store dumps were dotted all around the area and for those troops who had the time, and the money, Armentières, a short trip to the south, offered every kind of luxury available.

In the April of 1915, Lieutenant-Colonel V. F.

The church interior in early 1915.

Eberle then serving in the Plugstreet sector with the Royal Engineers remarked:

Our only change had been to move our Company Officer's billet to more comfortable quarters in a house (this was a row of small terraced houses in a main road in Plugstreet village).

In one of his many letters home, Lieutenant Ronald Poulton Palmer, 1/4th Royal Berkshire Regiment writes about being "placed in the local school close to the church", and the late Rifleman Tom Berry, 1st Battalion Rifle Brigade, recalled being billeted in private houses in the square as well as in the upper-

The schoolhouse in the village, Lieutenant Ronald Poulton Palmer's billet.

rooms of the estaminet Aux Trois Amis. On a visit to Plugstreet in the 1950s, he well remembered being warmly welcomed by the residents of this estaminet, then still trading as such, with the owner's wife recounting frequently in their conversation stories of "les boutons noirs", or "the black buttons", as the riflemen were nicknamed by the locals during the war, based on the colour of their uniform buttons.

The crossroads, Ploegsteert before the war with the two estaminets facing each other on opposite corners.

Ploegsteert crossroads in 2003. Aux trois Amis still there, with Café au Lion d'Or nowhere to be seen.

The Rifle Brigade enjoyed a special relationship with the Plugstreet residents, and an oft-repeated joke tells of a mustering in the main street when, at roll call, a certain Rifleman Smith didn't answer to the call. Rifleman Smith was well known in the battalion for his size 12 boots and a voice from the ranks, responding to a second call made by the sergeant-major, shouted out:

He won't be more than a moment Sarge, he's just marched down to the square to turn around!

Rifleman Aubrey Smith, 1st Battalion London Rifle Brigade, billeted in a barn on the outskirts of Plugstreet, wrote about his experience in the village in early 1915 thus:

What an absolute treat to sit down at a table again for a meal! We have our food cooked by the 'landlady' who also makes tea, and provides milk and won't hear of us using our enamelled plates, mugs or even knives and forks! No, she

provides crockery and cutlery and washes up afterwards and we feel quite at home. When back in civilised surroundings, it is very funny how a hair on our plate worries us, whereas we swallowed all manner of things in the barn.

Out of the village on the right of the road running south from the crossroads to Armentières, about 5–600 yards before where the brewery 'bath-house' was sited, stands London Rifle Brigade Cemetery. Just north of the cemetery was a nunnery school for girls, L'Ouvroir des Soeurs de Charité, used as the rest headquarters of 6th (Service) Battalion Royal Scots Fusiliers, 9th (Scottish) Division. In February 1916, it was graced with the presence of Battalion Commander Major, The Right Honourable Winston Spencer Churchill who, as a famous (or infamous?) ex-Cabinet Minister at the time, enjoyed a comfortable, well-furnished private office on the ground floor.

After the fiasco of the Gallipoli campaign, he had chosen to serve in the front line, spending a short time with the Grenadier Guards at Neuve Chapelle before taking command of the

Winston Churchill 'dressed to kill' in the French helmet that "helped prevent certain recognition".

5

6th Battalion, Royal Scots. The commanding officer he replaced was much admired by men and officers of the battalion alike, and one of the latter reflected on a popular feeling by commenting:

The bathhouse brewery south of Ploegsteert. Destroyed during the war, it was never rebuilt.

The houses now standing on the site of the old bathhouse brewery south of Ploegsteert.

Why could not Churchill have gone to the Argylls if he must have a Scottish regiment? We should all have been greatly interested to see him in a kilt.

Once taking over command of the battalion, this attitude soon changed as his boundless energy, attention to detail and his deep and honest concern for the welfare of his men became apparent. Such was the worth of the man that General Sir James Wilcocks said of him:

If I was a young man with life before me I would sooner serve with him than almost any man I know.

Churchill led the 6th Battalion of the regiment north from the Meteren Ridge to the Plugstreet area, where one of the guides assigned to showing the battalion officers around their new sector said to the adjutant:

Excuse me Sir, but your Commanding Officer is very like Mr Winston Churchill!

The adjutant agreed with the soldier replying that the resemblance had often been remarked upon. It was the adjutant's opinion that Churchill's habit of wearing a standard French-issue blue steel helmet helped prevent certain recognition.

At the nunnery school, referred to in his book *Thoughts and Adventures* as a convent and described by him and his colleagues as their 'tall, thin house', Churchill recounts being in his office proof-reading a secret document on caterpillar vehicles (later called Tanks), which had to be checked and returned directly to the Committee of Imperial Defence in London. While working on these and other documents the village came under heavy enemy bombardment. Looking out of the window which faced the enemy lines about a mile-and-a-half across the fields in front of the school, he noted that the shells were bursting in an ever-advancing line directly toward him. Deciding that a pane of glass between him and the advancing barrage did not constitute sound defence, he slipped out the back door to the battalion office in the next building, intending to shelter there until the shells passed. Unfortunately, Plugstreet then suffered one of the first of the methodical bombardments which would eventually bring it to near ruins. After an hour-and-a-half, all was silent and he returned to his office to find it totally destroyed. He collected his kit, belongings and papers noting that the all-important proofs were not amongst them. The room was swept and searched, everybody in the vicinity was questioned, but there was still no sign of his papers. Thoughts sprang to mind of spies among the civilians in the area. As the paper was marked in red ink: "This document is the property of His Majesty's Government", there was no doubt as to where would be its final destination if it did fall into the hands of a spy. Churchill was seriously alarmed, acutely anxious and, for the best part of three days, fretted over his incompetence. On the third day he put his hand into his inner breast-pocket, a pocket he rarely used, and there was the answer to his problems, his 'lost' secret proofs. In his book, he goes on to say what a pleasurable place his 'tall, thin house', and Plugstreet in general, became after his discovery.

L'Ouvroir des Soeurs de Charité, Winston Churchill's 'tall, thin house' before the war.

The site of L'Ouvroir des Soeurs de Charité, Winston Churchill's 'tall, thin house', today.

South of the hospice, just by London Rifle Brigade Cemetery, the River Warnave flows under the Armentières-Messines road and follows its lazy course across the field opposite. The track alongside the river was used by Churchill's 6th Royal Scots Fusiliers to reach their allotted positions in the trench lines at Le Gheer. Along the route south of the river were a number of shell-battered farmsteads bearing the names allotted them by previous battalions manning the area - Artillery Farm, London Farm, London Support Farm and Mountain Gun Farm, the last being named after a captured Austrian mountain-gun that was used at the farm to fire point-blank into the enemy trench lines around the convent at Le Gheer. The enemy didn't take kindly to this and his artillery gave the farm a good deal of attention causing the British to abandon it for good, but they continued to use it, and its nickname, as a map reference.

North of the river, Maison 1875, a farm named after a plaque built into its brickwork denoting the year it was built, was left completely untouched by German shelling, leading to a querying of the enemy's intention for it. Used as a billet and a mustering point by British regiments, the Germans must surely have known that it frequently housed troops.

Along the river to the east of Maison 1875, a small bridge over the River Warnave, McKenna's Bridge, was the main crossing point for the incoming and outgoing battalions trudging between trench and billet and vice-versa south of Plugstreet village. The track running north-east from this little bridge led to Laurence Farm, on some maps identified as Lawrence Farm. It was at this farm that Churchill set up the command post and forward battle headquarters of his battalion. It was also here that he used his battalion musicians to play in the farmyard hoping to provoke the Germans into retaliating to his own reaction to their musical performance of the day before. He had heard the strains of music coming from the German side of the line and immediately called down a barrage from the divisional artillery on the source of the sound, which effectively put an end to that particular performance. The following day Churchill assembled the battalion band who proceeded to give the Germans a rendering of Scottish airs and laments, while nervously awaiting the same sort of 'applause' as was handed out to the German musicians the day before. On receiving no reaction, Churchill commented:

So you see Gentlemen, either the Hun has no sense of humour or he actually likes Scottish music.

Due to his fame, Churchill was prone to receive visits from high-ranking officers and other dignitaries and it was from Laurence Farm that, after an evening entertaining the Divisional General, the Brigadier General on the General Staff of the Corps, two very distinguished flying officers, and the Divisional General's ADC, Churchill offered to take them for a tour of his battalion's trenches. This was obviously suggested for the benefit of the troops in the line who were rewarded with the sight and sounds of a senior group of men bedecked in the finery that befits their rank, stumbling and wallowing in the mud, getting hooked-up on the wire and generally experiencing conditions that were beyond their conception. It was little wonder that men of the 6th Royal Scots Fusiliers spoke of their commanding officer with deep affection during and after his period of serving with them.

Australian troops at Lancashire Support Farm in 1918.

The Convent at Le Gheer.

The track from Laurence Farm continued on to the ruined convent at Le Gheer, passing on its way, Lancashire Support Farm, named by men of the 1st East Lancs when it was used by them as a collecting point for materials to support their men in the line just a few hundred yards to the east. While the troops did their stints in the front-line around Le Gheer the whole length of this track would become a busy thoroughfare after dark, with men going about their business: sweating ration parties; jostling company messengers; and serious, grim-faced men engaged in the relief of the front-line troops treading their way carefully towards the trenches, slipping and sliding in the mud, until the stark, jagged ruins of the convent just south of Le Gheer crossroads would hove into view announcing that the front-line had been reached. Other relief parties with the same intent, but with their destination being the trenches further north along the eastern fringe of the wood, knew they were at the front when they passed the calvary at the crossroads in Le Gheer itself.

Providence smiled on this calvary, as it did with many on the Western Front. It survived the war and, now repaired, still sits on its corner at the crossroads. The convent at Le Gheer was rebuilt after the war, taking on a new rôle as an hospice, and many of the farms and dwellings in the area were rebuilt on their old sites. The flat meadows behind the convent where, in the war years two armies in opposing trench lines faced each other approximately a hundred yards apart, still become waterlogged and sodden during the winter months, and the incessant cold Flemish drizzle still transforms the area into an uncomfortable, damp and bone-chilling place to be.

No trace of Laurence Farm, Winston Churchill's old battalion headquarters, remains to be seen today other than a curve in the tractor-track where it once stood and a farm gate marking the entrance. Lancashire Support Farm was rebuilt a little north of its original position on the corner of the main path and the track that was used to access it. Both London Farm and London Support Farm are thriving, and Maison 1875 is a hive of agricultural activity still sitting just west of the river crossing that was McKenna's Bridge. The bridge no longer supports lines of men passing to and from trench line to billet, and the only transport now found crossing the River Warnave at this point is that of farm tractors moving between the fields.

Another much-used route to the trench lines around Le Gheer and east of the wood was the one along the Warneton road running north of the River Warnave and parallel to the southern edge of the wood. It runs east from the crossroads in Plugstreet village square to those at Le Gheer before continuing to Warneton. It was mostly regiments of the 4th Division who arrived in the area in October 1914 after their advance from the Marne and the Aisne in the south who established it as being the way to the front line. It was safe for troop movement during the dark hours, with men fanning out across the wet, sodden fields on either side of the road, stopping only when the dazzling glare of a Very light rose from the German lines to illuminate their path - and freeze their progress. Movement would have been slow and tortuous across these boggy meadows, all intersected with muddy, steep-sided brooks prone to break their banks when the rains came. 'Safety overrules discomfort' was the order of the day, and this was the safest way to get into the positions allotted them in the

London Farm in 1915.

The Calvary at Le Gheer crossroads as it was in 1915.

convent trench lines around Le Gheer and along the eastern edge of Plugstreet Wood itself, where a formidable German strongpoint, The Birdcage, embracing the cluster of houses of the hamlet Le Pelerin, dominated all.

On the left of the road, past the end of the built-up section lining the road as it leaves Plugstreet village is Touquet Berthe Farm, an important point of reference for incoming troops, an ideal spot for rations, general supplies, trench materials and ammunition to be collected on the way to the trenches. It was also used by some regiments as a reserve headquarters but its position in open ground led this practice to be discouraged. In spring 1918, when the Germans had secured the farm during their Lys Offensive, they started a burial plot there but no documentation is available to determine details of its presence or the number of burials. The British swept back and re occupied the area five months later, and in the post-war years, when the War Graves Commission went about its solemn task of gathering together the bodies of the fallen and establishing the permanent sites of military cemeteries, the plot was not deemed large enough to be left as a concentration of enemy graves. Consequentially the German bodies were relocated to other cemeteries in the area, but two unidentified RAF graves made in 1918 were moved to Strand Military Cemetery on the Armentières-Messines road.

Further along the road, on the right-hand side in the direction of Le Gheer, is a British military plot named Lancashire Cottage Cemetery which was started by men of the 1st Battalions of the East Lancashire and Hampshire Regiments. A small homestead facing it on the other side of the road, used as battalion headquarters and a dressing station by men of the East Lancs, gave its name to

the cemetery, and is one of the few war-destroyed buildings in the area that were never rebuilt in the post-war years. In the spring and summer of 1918 the Germans, as they did at Touquet Berthe Farm, started a burial plot at Lancashire Cottage Cemetery and these graves now make up part of it. North of Lancashire Cottage, within Plugstreet Wood, were two large farm complexes named by men of the Hampshire and Essex Regiments. Both would have been used for all manner of purposes by troops of these regiments. Hants Farm is still the centre of busy agricultural activity, but Essex Farm lies in ruins, with very little of them left to be seen, and with what is left of the farm's moat vainly trying to

The Calvary as it is today.

encircle them. This latter farm was within the treeline on the southern edge of the wood and its moat served as an important source of water for men serving within the wood during the war. A farmhouse replacing it was built on the Ploegsteert–Le Gheer roadside due south of its original position.

About a quarter-of-a-mile further along the road to the left stands a house at the main entrance to Plugstreet Wood giving access directly to Hunter Avenue, the main south-to-north ride through the wood. The line of small

New Zealanders building bivouacs along the western fringe of Plugstreet Wood.

The dugout complex in Plugstreet Wood along the Messines–Ploegsteert road.

concrete forts alongside Hunter Avenue were not considered safe enough to use as shelters by the troops, being used mainly as store housing. Further along the road, between Hunter Avenue and Le Gheer crossroads is the site of Keepers Hut, a wooden building and, like so many of them in the area, used as a battalion headquarters for various regiments or as a collecting point for materials supporting the troops in the line east of the wood and the hamlet of Le Gheer.

Activity along this road and the fields astride the River Warnave below it remained much the same as when Churchill and his Royal Scots had used them. However in late 1916, early 1917, troops of the Australian and New Zealand armies moved in and virtually occupied the neighbourhood of Ploegsteert. Frenzied activity commenced immediately on the western side of the wood, as men of the New Zealand Division began to build shelters, dugouts, bivouacs and regimental aid posts. Before long the area took on a different aspect. Bivouacs and sand-bagged dugouts lined the edges and the interior of the wood in preparation for a massive influx of troops. The reason became apparent when, just before midnight on 6 June, literally thousands of men traversed the area, moving northward instead of eastward. Everyone in the vicinity, and in the area to the north embracing the lower southern slopes of the Messines Ridge, including the Germans, well entrenched on their side of the line, would have been aware of this mass-movement of men, machines and horse and mule transports moving up to the front-line to play their part in an offensive planned to open in the very early hours of the following day.

Troops of the eight attack battalions of the 3rd Australian Division were on the move along four well-marked routes to their action fronts north of the wood in front of, and eastward along the line below La Petite Douve Farm stretching south-eastwards towards St. Yves. The Brown, Green, Blue and Red routes as they were designated, would lead the Australians from their camps and billets between Romarin and Pont de Nieppe across the River Warnave and over these fields, then up and on through the wood to their jumping-off positions in the trenches south of the village of Messines. Men from Regina Camp at Romarin, west of Plugstreet, followed the Brown Line, skirting north of the village square and crossroads before entering the western edge of the wood, then moving parallel with the Armentières-Messines road to their section of the front north of the wood. Troops following the Green Line left Oosthove Farm north of Armentières, trudging through the fields east of the village and entering the wood where a track between the village and Touquet Berthe Farm led to The Strand communication trench. Blue Line troops from Nieppe slogged across the fields and into the wood from a track at Touquet Berthe Farm itself, with those following the Red Line from Pont de Nieppe entering at another track between this farm and Lancashire Cottage, then on to Hants Farm from where they commenced their struggle through the wood – and all the time under constant bombardment.

This massive movement of men, horses, wagons, weaponry, ammunition and equipment in general saw officers and NCOs scurrying to and fro along the columns as they made their way along the designated rides and fire-alleys within the wood. They directed and encouraged the men to maintain pace and direction which they were carrying out under a tremendous enemy barrage of gas-, incendiary- and high-explosive shells persistently searching for them. The movement in the exploding-shell-flash-lit darkness of the wood was chaotic, with horses and mules slowing and obstructing the columns. Heavily burdened and struggling to breathe in the gas-laden wood, many of them just collapsed in their tracks gasping for breath in the poisonous air and causing havoc amongst the passing troops who themselves were half-blinded, struggling to maintain contact with the man in front, and finding it difficult to breathe due to their gas-masks. The effort of marching under these conditions while carrying rifle, ammunition, tools and rations, caused men to fall with fatigue and the disabling effect of the gas which would not disperse in the stagnant, still air of the wood.

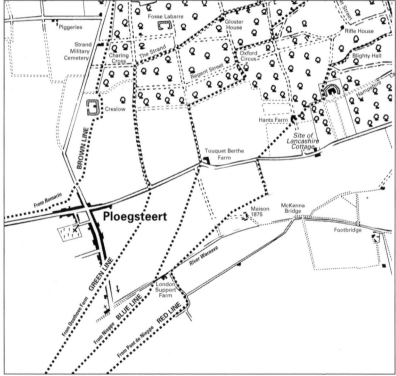

Routes taken by battalions of the 3rd Australian Division on 6 June 1917 when moving to their assembly points for the opening of the Messines offensive.

The progress of all four columns was slowed to such an extent that, at the time when the tails of the columns should have been deploying along their lines for the attack, the heads of the four columns were just leaving the wood. The clearer air outside the wood made all the difference and the Australians soon recovered, made up for lost time and gathered themselves in readiness for that which they had trained so hard. About 500 of them had been put out of action in the wood, most of them gassed, but the remainder, depleted in battalion strength as they were, assembled in their positions in full readiness for what was to come.

The medics in the specially concrete-constructed Regimental Aid Posts in the wood, preparing themselves to take care of the wounded from the forthcoming battle were suddenly overwhelmed with shell, gas and fatigue casualties. These were carried, or made their own way to the Australian support dugouts in Bunhill Row, a track alongside a small clearing on the northeast fringe of the wood, from where they were dispatched for treatment to the nearby Charing Cross Central Australian Dressing Station on the Ploegsteert–Messines road close to the western entrance of The Strand, the main communication trench that traversed the wood from west to east. This Dressing Station was experiencing its own problems, with the medical orderlies and doctors themselves wearing gas masks while frantically caring for the seemingly unending stream of casualties pouring in. Unable to effectively cope with the influx of the wounded, they were forced to redirect many of the walking and not so seriously wounded stretcher cases to be cared for by the New Zealand Advanced Dressing Station which was based at Underhill Farm alongside the Red Lodge road on the comparatively shellfire-free southern slopes of Hill 63.

In the meantime, the German artillery continued with its bombardment, while their infantry in their long established and well fortified entrenchments on the lower slopes of the southerly shoulder of the Messines Ridge, knowing what was approaching them, were apprehensive and fully aware that they were due, very shortly, to be attacked in strength – and they made their preparations accordingly.

What they did not know was that the opening phase of the attack would not be carried out by the mass of Australians troops mustering to their front. It would come from deep below, and in the very early morning of 7 June, 3.10 am to be exact, when four of the nineteen deep-tunnelled mines laid under German strongpoints along the ridge, would explode beneath them to signal the opening of the Messines Offensive.

When the mines did explode the last companies of the 3rd Australian Division were just leaving the wood, reaching their assembly positions, late, but ready to move forward. In two cases the men did not stop to muster on their allotted lines – they just carried on and advanced straight into No-Man's Land to join the attack.

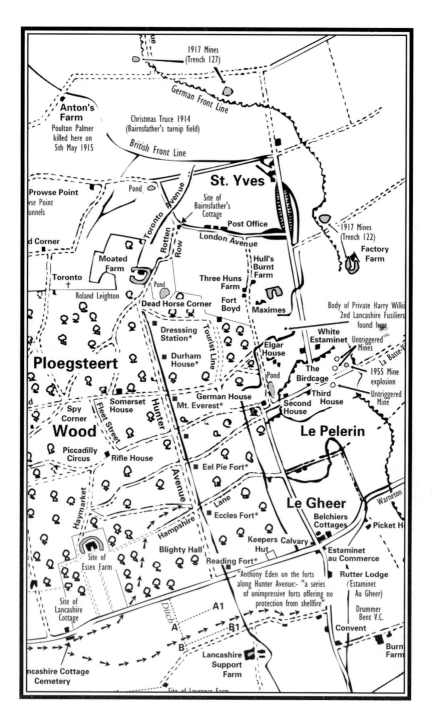

1917 Mines
(Trench 127)

German Front Line

Anton's Farm
Poulton Palmer killed here on 5th May 1915

Christmas Truce 1914
(Bairnsfather's turnip field)

British Front Line

Prowse Point
wse Point
unnels

Pond

St. Yves

Site of Bairnsfather's Cottage

Post Office

1917 Mines
(Trench 122)

d Corner

London Avenue

Factory Farm

Toronto Avenue

Rotten Row

Moated Farm

Hull's Burnt Farm

Toronto †

Roland Leighton

Pond

Three Huns Farm

Dead Horse Corner

Fort Boyd

Maximes

Body of Private Harry Wilki
2nd Lancashire Fusiliers
found here

Dresssing Station*

Tourist Line

White Estaminet

Untriggered Mines

La Basse-V

Ploegsteert

Durham House*

Elgar House

1955 Mine explosion

Pond

The Birdcage

Untriggered Mine

German House

Somerset House

Mt. Everest*

Third House

Second House

Le Pelerin

Spy Corner

Fleet Street

Hunter

Wood

Piccadilly Circus

Rifle House

Eel Pie Fort*

Avenue

Lane

Le Gheer

Warneton

Eccles Fort*

Belchiers Cottages

Picket H

Haymarket

Hampshire

Blighty Hall

Keepers Calvary Hut

Estaminet au Commerce

Reading Fort*

Site of Essex Farm

"Anthony Eden on the forts along Hunter Avenue:- "a series of unimpressive forts offering no protection from shellfire"

Rutter Lodge
(Estaminet Au Gheer)

Drummer Bent V.C.

A1

Site of Lancashire Cottage

Ditch

A'

B1

Convent

B'

Burn Farm

ncashire Cottage Cemetery

Lancashire Support Farm

Site of Laurence Farm

CHAPTER 2

LE GHEER TO ST. YVES

T HE LITTLE HAMLET OF LE GHEER with its convent, its crossroads' calvary and its estaminets, served to cater for the religious and thirst-quenching demands of the local agricultural communities tending the fields in this little backwater close to the Franco-Belgian border. In late October 1914, it was to find itself the centre of attention of a German army desperate to break the British line in its efforts to reach Calais. A soldier of the 4th Division was to say:

The enemy are being held by bluff, our line is just a fringe between the Germans and the sea.

To a point he was correct, but the 'fringe' was made up of the British Expeditionary Force which was in no mood to let the enemy have its way. Having failed to take Ypres and Armentières, the Germans focused their efforts on the sector between Messines and Armentières and launched attack after attack in a last-ditch attempt to meet their objective and pour through the thin British defences and onward to the coast. On 20 October they launched this offensive along the whole line stretching from La Bassée to the south and Menin to the north. Le Gheer happened to be just about in the middle of this line and was to take tremendous punishment before deadlock and winter halted the movement of both armies.

The 2nd Battalion Royal Inniskilling Fusiliers, 12th Brigade, 4th Division, moved into the area on 17 October and dug-in just east of Le Gheer, facing Pont Rouge, a border crossing between Belgium and France in enemy territory on the River Lys. Having seen action at Le Cateau, on the Marne, on the Aisne, at Meteren and, most recently, at Armentières, they were battle-hardened, though weary, having taken heavy casualties during their move north from France into Belgium. On 20 October, they beat off an attack by the Germans who were attempting to take Le Gheer which would have given them an important strategic advantage in breaking the line between Le Touquet in the south and Messines to the north. From this position, the Germans could lay down enfilade fire on the British 2nd Cavalry Brigade trenches along the eastern edge of the wood to the north, and those of the 12th Brigade, 4th Division to the south.

The road from Ploegsteert to Le Gheer, 1915.

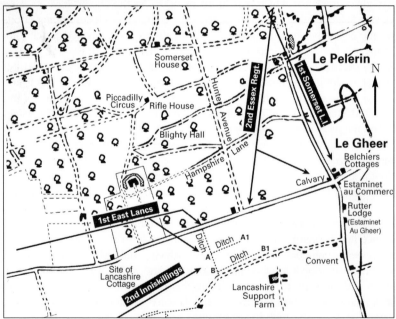

The attack on the German occupiers of Le Gheer, 21 October, 1914. The ditches marked A-A1, A-B and B-B1 were the German occupied 'trench' defences west of the village.

At 5.15 am the following day, a reinforced enemy attacked and forced the Royal Inniskillings to retire to a position about a quarter-of-a-mile westwards, back along the Ploegsteert–Warneton road. The Germans then occupied the hamlet and set up defences west of it in a ditch running south from the road and two others linking with it that ran parallel with the path leading from Laurence Farm to the Convent.

An immediate battle plan was put together by the British and there followed a classic joint action involving men of the 1st Battalions the East Lancashire Regiment and Somerset Light Infantry, both of the 11th Brigade, 4th Division, together with the 2nd Battalion Essex Regiment and the ousted 2nd Battalion Royal Inniskillings of the 12th Brigade. The Royal Inniskillings were now licking their wounds and smarting from their enforced exit from their recently held positions.

At 9 am the same morning of 21 October, two platoons of the 2nd Essex doubled through the wood from their positions in support of the 9th Lancers, 2nd Cavalry Brigade who were occupying trenches in what was shortly to become the German strongpoint named The Birdcage. One platoon took up a position facing Le Gheer while the other broke out on to the main Ploegsteert-Le Gheer road and surprised the Germans with enfilade fire as they lay in their ditches waiting for the situation to develop. Meanwhile, two companies of the East Lancs moved in from Ploegsteert along the edge of the wood, covered by the Inniskillings from positions in the open, south of the wood. The Somersets moved down the eastern edge from St. Yves, bayonet-charged the occupiers of Le Gheer and then effected a house-to-house search, clearing the hamlet of the enemy and cutting off the retreat of those of them now retiring from their defences to the west following the fierce onslaught of the East Lancs, Essex and Royal Inniskillings. The East Lancs, from just within the wood, had laid down devastating enfilade fire into the enemy defence line and, with the Royal Inniskillings advancing and giving covering fire, a platoon charged the enemy in trench A-A1, quickly overrunning them and causing them to flee in disarray. The German troops in trench A-B surrendered as soon as the charge began. Thus the enemy were removed from their recently gained positions. An account of the action from the 1st East Lancs battalion diary reads:

> The enemy put up a stout resistance; over two-thirds of the garrison of trench A-B were killed outright, and taking it all round, I think at least 50 per cent of the enemy in our vicinity were killed. There were not many wounded, and the proportion of killed to wounded was abnormally high.

By the afternoon of 21 October the situation was retrieved. The East Lancs took over the recovered trenches east of Le Gheer with the battalion headquarters being set up in the Estaminet au Commerce on the corner of the crossroads. forty-five men of all ranks of the Inniskillings, taken prisoner in the earlier action, were released and 134 German prisoners were taken. German losses were estimated at about a thousand and in the next few days over 300 of their dead were buried in and around Le Gheer. (During the Christmas Truce of that year another 100 were buried in No-Man's Land). Although successful, this little action had cost the already depleted 2nd Battalion Royal Inniskillings dearly, having taken casualties of six killed and 16 wounded in the original attack and the ferocity of the counter-attack cost them three officers and 33 other ranks killed and three officers and 16 other ranks wounded.

A prelude to this action was recounted by Lieutenant Colonel N.G. Thwaites, 4th Dragoon Guards. He tells of Lieutenant R.G. Fetherstonehaugh of the 4th Dragoons, riding a bicycle into the village following an instruction to make contact with the Royal Inniskillings. On his way he noticed what he thought was a German prisoner sleeping by the road. Another 100 yards on he came across three German officers, hands in pockets and smoking cigarettes, in the middle of the road. The penny dropped, he quickly dismounted, turned his bicycle around and pedalled as fast as he could back to where he had come from, again passing the 'sleeping prisoner' who started taking pot-shots at him. Later, when the Somersets moved through the wood for their attack, he noted:

> Then, without warning, a trickle of sweating, cursing but quite good-tempered lads came through the woods behind us. They seemed to know what was expected of them, for at the edge of the wood, and without pausing, they fixed bayonets, and, as one of our men said, vulgarly, went through the village of Le Gheer and the Boche occupiers 'like a dose of salts' ... Presently a stream of wounded men began to trickle back to the cover of the woods. A man bearing on his back a wounded comrade, a young officer with a painful wound through the forearm, and another with a smashed finger, both of whom refused to be dressed until all their men were seen to. One poor fellow seemed to have stopped half a dozen fragments of shrapnel with his face; another had been caught by a burst of machine-gun bullets. They moaned pitifully until the ambulance man gave them a shot of something in the arm. The edge of the wood became an advanced dressing station. It looked like a slaughter house. Meanwhile, in the village the Hun was having a rough time. He was quite unprepared for an attack from this side, and the Somerset lads were in the main street before the Germans were aware of their danger. Trench after trench was taken, the British bayonets doing savage work that hot evening. Heaps of Germans filled the dug-outs on the edge of the village, and when we got to the far side the enemy was on the run.

For the rest of the month and well into November the enemy kept up his bombardment all along the line, interspersed with frequent infantry attacks, but to no avail, the 'fringe' manning the front-line held. Sir John French's despatch of the 14 November referring to this offensive read:

> I fully realised the difficult task which lay before us and the onerous rôle which the British Army was called upon to fulfil. That success has been attained, and all the enemy's desperate attempts to break through our line frustrated, is due to the marvellous fighting power and the indomitable courage and tenacity of

officers, non-commissioned officers and men. No more arduous task has ever been assigned to British soldiers and in all their splendid history there is no instance of their having answered so magnificently to the desperate calls which of necessity were made of them.

During this period, just behind the convent ruins at Le Gheer on 3 November, Drummer Spencer John Bent, 1st Battalion East Lancashire Regiment, performed the final act culminating in his being awarded the Victoria Cross. The 4th Division had taken over the line from the right flank of the 1st Cavalry Division and, during the previous days' actions, Drummer Bent had been conspicuous in his acts of bravery. At daybreak on 3 November the East Lancashire trenches, under heavy bombardment, were being systematically destroyed. In No-Man's Land several men were lying wounded in the open and Drummer Bent, ignoring the shelling, crawled out in an effort to bring them back to the safety of the British line. One of them, Private J. McNulty, lay about 30-yards from the trench line and the gallant Bent, slipping and sliding about, fell over in his effort to lift the wounded man onto his back. Shells and bullets helped him decide to stay down, so he hooked his feet under Private McNulty's armpits and back-crawled to the British trenches dragging the wounded man with him. Bent suffered wounds to his legs, arms, hands and head and was sent back to England to recover. He was awarded the Victoria Cross in December 1914, receiving it from King George V at Buckingham Palace on 13 January 1915. His citation in the London Gazette, 9 December, 1914 was published as:

Drummer Spencer John Bent VC, 1st East Lancs Regt.

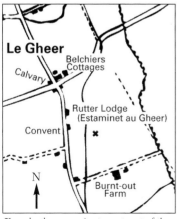

Le Gheer

Belchiers Cottages

Calvary

Rutter Lodge (Estaminet au Gheer)

Convent

N

Burnt-out Farm

X marks the approximate spot east of the convent in No-Man's Land from where Drummer Bent back-crawled Private McNulty to safety.

Spencer John Bent, No. 8581, Drummer, 1st Battn. the East Lancashire Regt. Date of act of bravery: 1-2 Nov. 1914. For conspicuous gallantry near Le Gheir (sic), on the night of 1-2 Nov., when, after his officer, platoon sergeant and section commander had been struck down, he took command, and with great presence of mind and coolness succeeded in holding the position. Drummer Bent had previously distinguished himself on two occasions, 22 and 24 Oct., by bringing up ammunition, under heavy shell and rifle fire, and again on the 3 Nov., when he brought into cover some wounded men who were lying exposed in the open.

He was later awarded the Cross of St. George 3rd Class by the Emperor of Russia.

After recovering from his wounds he continued serving, eventually being promoted to Regimental Sergeant-Major with the 1st Battalion. In October 1918, he was awarded the Military Medal for his involvement in critical patrolling activities in France. He survived the war and continued to serve as a peacetime soldier, retiring in 1926 after 21-years' service as Warrant Officer Class 2, Company Sergeant Major S. J. Bent, VC, MM. He died peacefully in London on 3 May 1977 at the age of 86.

On the corner of the Le Gheer cross-roads, opposite the calvary, is a group of dwellings named at the time Belchier Cottages, a misspelling of Belcher.

Lance-Sergeant Douglas Walter Belcher, 1st Battalion London Rifle Brigade had used these cottages as a *matériels* dump for pioneering workers of the battalion during the winter of 1914 and the troops, accordingly, named the cottages after him. He made a name for himself worthy of more than a group of cottages when he was awarded the Victoria Cross while holding firm against continuous German attacks on Mousetrap Farm east of Boesinghe during the Second Battle of Ypres. It was claimed at the time that he

Lance-Sergeant Douglas Belcher having a snack. had held, and saved, the flank of the whole 4th Division single-handedly. Douglas Walter Belcher ended the war as an acting-captain, returning to Surrey where he died of natural causes in 1953.

Passing Belchier Cottages on the right, the road heading directly north from the cross-roads follows the edge of the wood in what was No-Man's Land, with

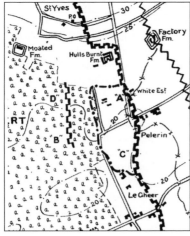

the British front-line running parallel to it inside the fringe of the wood. A right-angled bend turns eastwards into a small hamlet called Le Pelerin, the old area of The Birdcage, then a sprawling complex of defensive trenches and dugouts taken by the Germans in the November 1914 actions and developed into a heavily-fortified strongpoint. It formed its own salient, nosing into the British line between Le Gheer to the south and St. Yves to the north, creating what commanders of the British 4th Division, then holding the area, described as a "Bight in their (the German) Line". It was heavily wired and

The Birdcage, November 1914.

prompted early British units to describe it as a 'Birdcage', a name it kept for the rest of the war.

Just within the wood, at the tip of the right-hand turn in the road from Le Gheer, was a German observation and sniper post named, without much imagination but for obvious reasons, German House. It was sometimes referred to as First House being the first of three houses in a line along the short section of road extending north-eastwards into The Birdcage itself. The other two houses were named, not surprisingly, Second House and Third House, and sometimes Second and Third German House respectively.

On 19 December 1914, units of the 11th Infantry Brigade, 4th Division, attacked The Birdcage with the objectives of keeping enemy troops from being moved down as reserves to meet an attack by the French at Arras in France. The plan was for the 1st Battalion Rifle Brigade to take German House, Second House and the road running north-east into The Birdcage and capture the enemy defences there – the Rifle Brigade referred to their part in the raid as an attack on the "German House defences". The 1st Battalion Somerset Light Infantry would attack on the left flank of the Rifle Brigade and take the enemy breastworks facing them, and the 1st Battalion Hampshire Regiment would keep down enemy fire to the right of the Rifle Brigade, while manning the gap between the north end of Hampshire Trench and The Birdcage, moving its left-of-line forward to conform with the advance of the Rifle Brigade once the attack was completed successfully.

The enemy wire in front of the Somersets was about six-feet high and six-feet deep and the ground they had to cross was almost impassable, covered

with gaping shell-holes filled with water and slimy mud. The Somersets had prepared 'mattresses' from straw and rabbit wire which were to be thrown on the wire, enabling the men to cross without getting hooked up. The attack was launched, and failed in most of its objectives, with the British incurring heavy casualties with no tangible results other than capturing and retaining German House, destroying Second House and driving the enemy out of what little of the wood it held, moving their own front-line to the edge of the wood and on to the Le Gheer–St. Yves road.

The attackers had come under heavy machine-gun and rifle fire from the start and remained under it while trying to cross the slimy, muddy, shell-holed, wire-entangled ground.

German House 1914.

Captain the Hon Richard George Grenville Morgan Grenville.

The Rifle Brigade lost their lead officer immediately, Captain the Hon Richard George Grenville Morgan Grenville being killed by a shot from Third House as he and his men dashed out of the wood. The platoon to their left was checked by the state of the ground, heavy German machine-gun fire and 'shorts' from the British artillery; the supporting platoon, moving from the wood's edge was stopped, taking punishment from its own artillery and Second Lieutenant Archibald Stewart Lindsey Daniell and every man in his party, were killed when moving left of the main attack in an effort to make contact with the Somersets. The attack floundered after an hour and an attempt to organise a renewal of it resulted in the death of Captain the Hon Francis Prittie, second-in-command of the battalion. The Rifle Brigade, Somersets and Hampshires all took casualties from their

Second Lieut. Archibald Stewart Lindsey Daniell.

Captain the Hon Francis Reginald Denis Prittie.

own shell-fire which had failed to keep the Germans' heads down. The casualty call for the Rifle Brigade was three officers and 23 other ranks killed and three officers and 43 other ranks wounded. The Somersets had succeeded in taking the enemy line facing them, having made their way forward under German machine-gun fire, with their own artillery shells falling on them. Captains C. C. Maud,

Men of the 1st Battalion Rifle Brigade manning breastworks in Plugstreet Wood in 1914.

26

Captain R. C. Orr.   Captain C. C. Maud.   Captain F. S. Bradshaw.   Lieut. G. R. Parr.

R. C. Orr and F. S. Bradshaw and Lieutenants G. R. Parr and S. B. Henson were killed, one officer wounded and taken prisoner and 27 other ranks killed, 50 wounded and 30 missing. The 1st Hampshires' lost one officer, Major G. H. Parker, and 15 other ranks killed and one officer and 25 other ranks wounded. A note in their battalion diary's on the action reads:

> This attack was really stopped by our own guns

Lieut. S. B. Henson.   Immediately after the attack, the Rifle Brigade set about burying their dead:

Major G. H. Parker

> Sunday afternoon we were burying the dead in the wood, three-and-a-half feet (depth of grave) - some in a foot of water

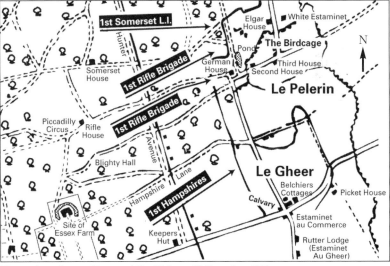

The attack on German House and The Birdcage, 19 December, 1914.

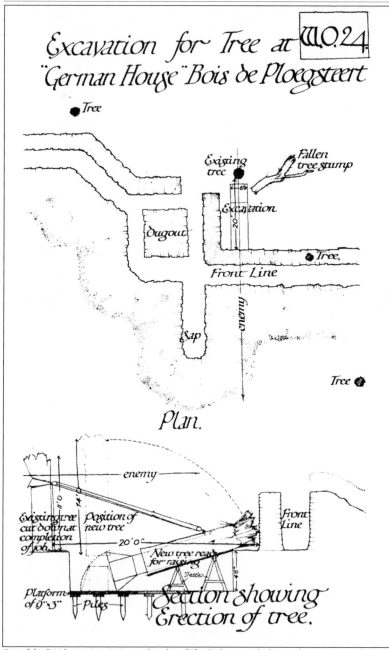

Excavation for Tree at W.O.24

"German House" Bois de Ploegsteert

Tree

Existing tree

Fallen tree stump

Excavation

Dugout

Tree,

front Line

enemy

Sap

Tree

Plan.

enemy

Existing tree cut down at completion of job.

Position of new tree

front Line

New tree ready for raising

Trestles

Platform of 9'·3"

Piles

20'·0"

Section showing Erection of tree.

One of the British Army's activities on the edge of The Birdcage resulted in an observation post disguised as a tree.

They re-established their front line, building a new line of breastworks inside the edge of the wood around German House, but consistent German gunfire caused this work to run into the early months of 1915 before it was finished. Although these breastworks were meant to be concealed from enemy eyes by the tree line, one of the soldiers describing the work wrote:

> The front of the wood got thinner and thinner as the Germans shelled and dead wood fell away, and the screening of our breastworks became difficult.

After this abortive attack no more attempts were made to take The Birdcage, nor did the Germans try to eject the British from the wood until their spring offensive in 1918. Small raids were carried out frequently by both the British

O.P. IN PLOEGSTEERT WOOD AT U-21.b.26.25. (Sheet 28)

Description.

A stump of oak to hold observer. 11 feet high 2 ft 2 ins diameter. Approach through PLOEGSTEERT Wood Trench railway near. Ground broken and boggy About 20 Feet from Front Line trench It is proposed to increase the height of the tree by 3 feet as it is important to obtain good observation, and to increase the height of the parapet accordingly: latter work to be done by occupants

TREE

Front Line Trench

View from S.E.

The map reference places it just on the edge of The Birdcage fringing the wood north of German House.

Members of the local community inspecting the crater left by the exploded mine in 1955.

and the Germans and each developed sniping to a fine art. Apart from regular shelling the area remained quiet, with both sides using it to instruct incoming units in trench life acclimatisation and the techniques of static warfare.

No traces of German House or Second House remain today other than the earth and vegetation-covered footings of the former just within the wood. Third House was rebuilt on its original site where the road in Le Pelerin turns sharply left at a fork within what was The Birdcage. The left hand fork runs northwards toward St. Yves while the right-hand one leads straight on, in an easterly direction, toward La Basse-Ville, another small hamlet on the way to Warneton.

A little way along this road, in the field to the right, is a slight depression, only visible in rainy weather when the crop is down and water has gathered on its indented surface. This harmless-looking 'puddle' marks the spot where a deep-tunnelled mine lies dormant. One of a pair tunnelled in for the opening of the Battle of Messines, its sister mine, in the field to the left-hand side of the road, was triggered by lightning striking a nearby electricity pylon during a heavy thunderstorm in the summer of 1955. After thirty-eight years of inactivity, it had roared into life, reminding the local population of how unpopular had been the previous occupants of this area. A large section of the land disappeared and was immediately replaced with a massive crater but, fortunately, there were no casualties and the local authorities quickly repaired the damage. Four mines, laid in two pairs, with the intent of eliminating the menace of The Birdcage, were left dormant following the Messines offensive in June 1917. Apart from the one beneath the 'puddle' in the field to the right, another pair lay beneath the field on the left, nearby the one that was triggered in 1955. So

The water-filled depression in the field identifies the site of the sister to the mine that exploded in 1955. Plugstreet Wood is in the background with the road from Warneton on the right.

The Factory Farm crater in 1919.

An upturned German bunker found in the Factory Farm crater.

one of the four has gone but the other three are still there, and who knows what the future holds for them? Whether or not the local community is aware that three more of these subterranean monsters still lie beneath its land is not clearly apparent.

One of these well could be the mine mentioned in the Argyll and Sutherland Highlanders' account stating:

> A tunnel was dug by the Tunnelling Company from our front-line to The Birdcage which was a system of trenches in the enemy's support line and so powerfully was it charged it was expected that no men in The Birdcage would escape. Our men used to carry up the ammonal at night in boxes which were popularly known by the men as 'Chocolate Boxes'. The secret of the mine was wonderfully kept and though we had a shrewd idea of what was going on not a word of it was mentioned. It is doubtful whether this mine was ever blown. Unkind people used to say that as soon as we placed the ammonal in the mine the Boche used to take it out from the other end!

Originally twenty-four mines were laid for the offensive, mostly in pairs under strongpoints all along the line from Hill 60 to just south of Messines. On the day, 7 June 1917, only nineteen made their presence known. Of the remaining five, one destined to eliminate La Petite Douve Farm was abandoned, its galleries and chamber flooded after the enemy became aware of its presence and destroyed part of the workings.

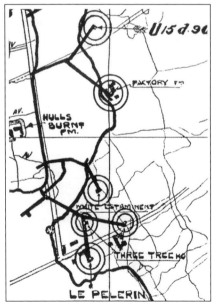

The two Factory Farm mines, the most southerly blown, and the four untriggered mines tunnelled-in under The Birdcage.

The other four, tunnelled in below The Birdcage were left dormant because British High Command had decided that enemy reserves would be closer to the resulting craters than the attackers and might well occupy them and play havoc with the oncoming infantry. It was therefore decided not to fire them but to keep them charged for possible use in later operations. As it was, they were never used.

Col. H. Stewart, CMG, DSO, MC in his comprehensive work, *The Official History of New Zealand Division's Effort in the Great War, Vol II, France*, notes:

In all, twenty-four mines were constructed, four of which were outside the front ultimately selected for our offensive.

The Australian historian, Dr. C. E. W. Bean writes in *The Official History of Australia in the War of 1914-18, volume IV, The A.I.F. in France 1917*:

By the date of the battle, twenty-three deep mines had been tunnelled beneath the German front line ... The British also had four mines ready charged beneath 'The Birdcage' (Le Pelerin), 400 yards further south. It was at first intended to explode these also, but this decision was altered. If the mines were fired, the craters might be useful to the enemy, whereas if they were kept ready to fire they might greatly assist a later operation. In the end, owing to the subsequent German retirement, they were not fired.

It seems odd, and a little irresponsible, that devices capable of such destruction should be left untouched, or maybe forgotten – which poses the question: "What has been done about the other three since 1955?"

The British front-line continues north along the edge of the wood passing a gathering of trees in a field on the right of the Le Gheer–St. Yves road. Further north of this apparent copse, on a rise behind it, is another. Both, in fact, border large water-filled mine craters, the sole reminders of what happened to a farm, its moat and its adjoining complex of buildings when 40,000 pounds of ammonal was buried 60 feet below it and then exploded. Identified as Factory Farm by British troops in the early years of the war, it was the centre of a well-fortified German strongpoint. It, with many others, disappeared with the blowing of the mines heralding the opening of the Battle of Messines in 1917.

These two, the most southerly exploded, were driven-in from Trench 122 by the 171st Tunnelling Company. It was in the upward-sloping escape-tunnel running from the foot of the main shaft that Lieutenants Cecil Hall and George Dickson were to trigger the mines. On the afternoon of 6 June, Hall received orders that the triggering would be from an adjoining trench, not the escape-tunnel. This meant extending twelve firing-wires 70 feet from the bottom of the tunnel and, as Lieutenant Dickson was in a dugout recovering from the effect of gas shells then falling in the wood, Hall did the job himself, a hard task considering he was wearing a gas mask. He worked through the night finishing only at 2.50 am the next day. 15-minutes later, his completed task helped obliterate a German strongpoint, preparing the ground for the growth of those two clumps of trees.

Trench 122 lay alongside the main road, due south of a small road branching right. This road finds its way between the two craters which now exist for watering cattle or a little private fishing. It is difficult to imagine the scene that met the eyes of the men of the 171st Tunnelling Company, a vast, mass of wire entanglements and trenches cluttering the field between them and the farm. It is even more difficult to imagine the sight, and the sound, at 3.10 am that June morning in 1917, the exact time that Lieutenants Hall and Dickson's triggering obliterated Factory Farm for all time.

From Trench 122, the line continued north to the edge of the St. Yves Ridge. Made up of two hills rising to 35 metres, it offered excellent observation over the enemy lines opposite in the valley of the River Douve. On the left, a turning leads through the hamlet of St. Yves, a small clustering of dwellings which, during the war, was a gathering of ruined cottages and buildings. It was totally destroyed in a critical week in October 1914 when the 1st Battalion Somerset Light Infantry held the line from Le Gheer to the River Douve. They had played their part well in clearing the Germans from Le Gheer on 21 October before taking over this part of the line the same evening. They set up their headquarters in an estaminet which, on the morning of 22 October, became a mass of ruins as St. Yves was heavily shelled. Headquarters moved to the cellars of another building and it, in turn, was demolished. Eventually, they moved to a building on the eastern exit of the hamlet while the enemy continued to pound the whole area on and off throughout the week. The weather broke and the rains came, causing the Somersets to record that their trenches were:

... an absolute quagmire with mud and filth on all sides.

They were relieved on 28 October, retiring to the second line of trenches near Hill 63 when the Battle for Armentières and the First Battle of Ypres were being fought simultaneously. This was the week:

... the worst so far spent by the Battalion.

A German breakthrough on the Messines–Ploegsteert front would have had disastrous effects on the British army, allowing the enemy to outflank Armentières from the north, a decisive move in their drive for Calais. The breakthrough didn't happen, but the total destruction of St. Yves did.

When the the lines set-in for the duration, many of those ruined buildings were used as observation posts or forward billets for officers. Those of the building that housed the post office, took to its new rôle and became a trench map reference, known to all and sundry as - the Post Office! Others were given such names as Bubble House, Dublin Castle, Warwick Castle, Machine Gun House and Lone House. One of them, The Nick, just left of Westminster Avenue (a support trench running from below Prowse Point eastward across Rotten Row, then linking with London Avenue), earned its name by a) being sited in a 'nick' between two fallen trees, b) because everything used to build it had been 'nicked' and c) the soldier most responsible for its construction was a Lance Corporal Nicholls of the Royal West Kents, better known as 'Nick', .

One wall of the Post Office backed a trench system where, in late December 1916, an officer serving with the Cheshire Regiment recorded the 10-second anguish of a fellow officer who shared his dugout. He was woken by shell explosions in the middle of the night to find his companion sitting on the edge of his bunk with his head in his hands, a finger pushed firmly in each ear, nodding his head and upper body to and fro and slowly counting to ten. When he reached the count of ten he jumped up from his bunk and rushed out, followed by the now wide-awake officer. Once outside, he climbed over the dugout beckoning his fellow officer to follow and pointed to an unexploded

Minenwerfer, "as big as a cask", standing upright, split down the middle, against a wall of sandbags approximately two yards away from where the ten-second count had been made inside the dugout. They quickly collected the detonator and returned to catch-up on their night's sleep. At noon the next day, the '10-second' officer left for his Christmas leave, no doubt reflecting on what might have been if he had been unable to finish his count.

Once the trench lines established themselves after the 1914 battles, the St. Yves Ridge was classified as being on the most southerly tip of the front line in Belgium, retaining its importance as an area for observation. Second Lieutenant R. B. Talbot Kelly, 52nd Brigade Royal Field Artillery, describes the observation posts on the St. Yves Ridge as:

> ... the last word in front-line luxury. Under the broken buildings we lived by night in secure and well-furnished cellars, sleeping in wire bunks of the best.

Many of these posts were important enough to be used exclusively for observation so as to avoid being detected by the enemy, their use for billeting, headquarters or as firing bays being disallowed. They were invariably in the front-line, approached through small tunnels under the trench parapets and by concealed saps. One such was the Crow's Nest just east of St. Yves Avenue (London Avenue as featured on some trench maps), used primarily to observe enemy activities in the area of The Birdcage. Many regiments serving here-abouts would base their headquarters in the farm track named Rotten Row alongside Machine Gun House (later to achieve lasting fame as Bruce Bairnsfather's cottage), or near Dead Horse Corner and Hull's Burnt Farm, all in a sunken track area on the downwards slope leading directly into the wood, well shielded from curious enemy eyes. However, there were other contestants to worry about. The whole area, as was Plugstreet Wood itself, well deserved its reputation for being rat-infested:

> ... fat, domesticated rats which, we were led to believe, were still living on the bully and biscuits buried in the neighbourhood in 1915! One thing is certain, they thrived on their diet whatever it was, for they were enormous specimens, especially those in the support line around the ruins of Hull's Burnt Farm, where the officers used surreptitiously to expend quantities of revolver ammunition and the men got in a deal of bayonet practice.

One officer experiencing a problem with rats decided to do something about it and, on returning from leave, brought back with him two ferrets. When asking for someone to look after them, one of his company signallers volunteered immediately and, on being questioned as to his knowledge of fer-rets, responded, in a slightly offended manner: "I am a poacher by profession Sir!" The poacher and his new-found wards earned their keep and on one occasion alone were recorded as having 'bagged' over a 100 rats. The Germans also contributed to keeping down the rat count as the 10th Battalion Argyll and Sutherland Highlanders' history records:

LE GHEER TO ST. YVES

We were infested with rats and one day a whizzbang landed just behind 'A' Company H.Q. in a bit of ground known as the 'Flower Garden' but which was in reality a horrible mass of mud, the result being that a large number of rats were uprooted and killed. That night, in the casualty wire to the Adjutant, the return sent in read: 'Casualties. Rats - 36 killed, 28 wounded, more wounded coming in.

The C.O. thinking we had had a catastrophe, and not at first observing the word 'rats' which was in small letters, was highly perturbed

The front-lines in this area were in some places only 75-100 yards apart. Both sides took to posting notice boards with messages intended to irritate, intimidate, or just to inform the opposition as to how much they knew about them. The Germans often 'welcomed' British regiments into the line showing they knew exactly who was facing them and regularly quoted names of commanding officers. This gave rise to concern about a spy-network among the civilians behind British lines. This 'word-warfare' had a lighter side, shown when the Germans put up a board in No-Man's Land, close to their wire with: "Where is your wonderful British navy?" written on it. This was following the sinking of a number of British ships. Men of the Cameron Highlanders in the line at the time sent out a party during the night and brought back the board, substituting it with one of their own with the message:

Where is your wonderful notice-board?

Canadian troops rat catching in Plugstreet Wood in 1915.

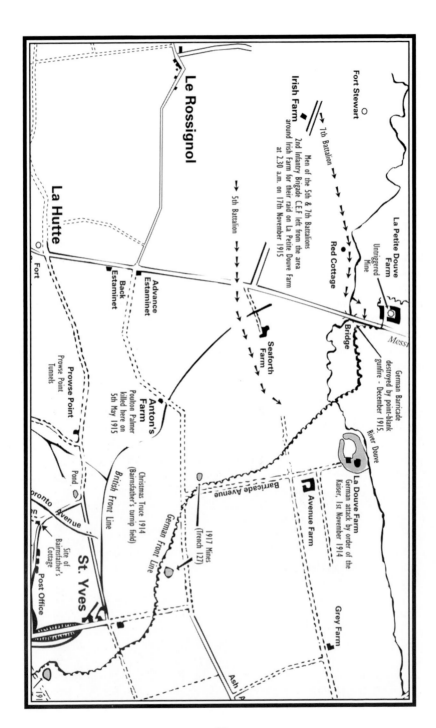

Fort Stewart

Irish Farm

7th Battalion

Men of the 5th & 7th Battalions
2nd Infantry Brigade C.E.F. left from the area
around Irish Farm for their raid on La Petite Douve Farm
at 2.30 a.m. on 17th November 1915

Le Rossignol

5th Battalion

La Hutte

Fort

Advance
Estaminet

Back
Estaminet

Seaforth
Farm

La Petite Douve
Farm
Untriggered
Mine

Red Cottage

Bridge

Mess

German Barricade
destroyed by point-blank
gunfire - December 1915.

River Douve

La Douve Farm
German attack by order of the
Kaiser, 1st November 1914

Avenue
Farm

Barricade Avenue

Grey Farm

Ash

Prowse Point
Prowse Point
Tunnels

Anton's
Farm
Poulton Palmer
killed here on
5th May 1915

Pond

British Front Line

Christmas Truce 1914
(Bairnsfather's turnip field)

German Front Line

1917 Mines
(Trench 127)

oronto
en
Avenue

Site of
Bairnsfather's
Cottage

St. Yves

Post Office

191

38

CHAPTER 3

ST. YVES TO LA HUTTE

THE ST. YVES RIDGE WAS ALSO USED extensively for the siting of machine-gun posts. A lieutenant of the 1st Battalion Royal Warwickshire Regiment, 4th Division, acting as machine-gun officer in the area, made quite a name for himself with his sardonic sense of humour and his talent for impromptu sketching. Trudging along the wet and tortuous route around his machine-gun positions on and around the ridge on many a dark and lonely night, Lieutenant Bruce Bairnsfather fostered a germ of an idea which was to change the course of humour in the war and dramatically affect his life and circumstances.

His route back to his dugout took him past the ruined cottages in St. Yves which housed some of his fellow officers. He yearned to enjoy a little of that elusive condition called comfort, and fate showed its hand for him one day when an officer offered to share one of the cottages with him (this one was known by the troops as Machine Gun House). Bairnsfather soon settled himself into his new billet, and, between stints of duty and during the long boring hours when moving about in the open was considered a sure way to a quick grave, he was soon busy sketching. Humourous situations depicting Tommy's misery and discomfort, the belief that the entire German army was dedicated to removing him from the face of the earth, and many other subjects close to the soldier's heart, were drawn on all sorts of scrap paper, the cottage walls, and any suitable material that came to hand. These little works became popular with the troops and he soon earned himself a reputation as his scraps of paper, through popular demand, found their way along the trench lines.

The ruins of his cottage billet completely disappeared in the post-war years but today a post-war-built house marks the corner spot where he developed his 'germ of an idea' into a world famous character. Sitting on the curve of the road through St. Yves, it marks the spot where a character with a walrus moustache and tousled hair under a battered cap was born; the character who would stand up for the ordinary bloke in khaki who felt the whole world had picked on him – and so arose from the Flanders mud the figure of Old Bill. Soon after the 1914 Christmas Truce, Old Bill drawings and other illustrations began to appear on the walls of cottages, barns and dugouts in the area of St. Yves and much farther afield. In August 1915, the 15th Battalion 48th Highlanders of

A Bruce Bairnsfather illustration of Plugstreet Wood.

Canada who used Ration Farm north of Hill 63 as its Battalion H.Q., described the farm as:

> ... a group of uninhabited buildings, slightly blown, where cartoons by Bairnsfather were found on the walls. They were in charcoal and every battalion helped to preserve them

An engineer officer visiting the farm which had at one time been the front-line headquarters of the Warwickshire Regiment noted:

> On the whitewashed walls some previous artist among the British occupants had drawn, almost life-size in charcoal, delightful sketches of the Dame Gibson Girl type, and copies of La Vie Parisienne drawings. The drawings referred to were by Bruce Bairnsfather who had been at the farm.

Old Bill would be depicted in commonplace happenings to the soldier in the line - a shell-burst forcing the occupants of the cottage to run for cover; a near miss from a sniper; the qualities inherent in army issue biscuits; comments of men on fatigues, or remarks on an order they felt wasn't what it should be. The shell-burst sketch captioned "Where did that one go?" was he sent to *The Bystander* magazine in London. To his surprise, he received a letter from the magazine editor saying 'We like it, here's a cheque for two pounds, do you have any more, we'd be pleased to receive them?'. He set about sketching Old Bill's reaction to a sniper's near-miss and then a scenario involving army biscuits. These he captioned respectively: "They've evidently seen me!" and "Chuck us the biscuits Bill – the fire needs mending!" and sent them off. He was soon a regular contributor to *The Bystander* resulting in the magazine issuing a series of publications for the general public dedicated to Old Bill.

The 1st Royal Warwicks eventually left the Plugstreet sector and marched northward into the Second Battle of Ypres where Bairnsfather was wounded on 24 April 1915, a day which saw his regiment lose over 500 officers and men. He was invalided to England, having contributed to the final victory by letting loose Old Bill on the battlefields of France and Flanders.

His own description of Old Bill can hardly be bettered:

First discovered in the alluvial deposits
of southern Flanders.
Feeds almost exclusively on jam
and water biscuits.
Hobby: Filling sandbags,
on dark and rainy nights.

Lieutenant Bruce Bairnsfather standing alongside 'his' pond on Christmas Day 1914.

As the road passes Bairnsfather's cottage site, it climbs a small rise and then turns sharply left. In his book *Bullets & Billets*, Bairnsfather features a photograph of himself standing in front of a pond. The pond is still there today in the corner where the road makes its left turn. Directly facing is a field, a waterlogged turnip field in December 1914. The British front-line used to run west to east through it, although the major part of the field was No-Man's Land. During the Christmas Truce of 1914, men of both armies in this part of the line met here to talk together, swap souvenirs and cigarettes and were said to have played a game of football together before returning to their lines to get on with the war. Both sides took the opportunity during the cessation of hostilities to recover their dead from No-Man's Land:

The wood had taken a hell of a fight, and only during the Christmas Truce could many of the bodies be buried. So they are buried very shallow, and in about a month it should be pretty evil. As it is it stinks abominably and close to our advanced work there is a poor fellow only half-buried with his bayonet scabbard sticking out.

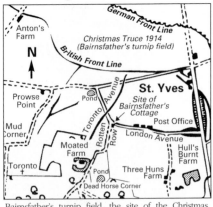

Bairnsfather's turnip field, the site of the Christmas Truce and football match in the area north of Plugstreet Wood, 1914.

Although this gathering of bodies also happened in the area of The Birdcage, for some reason the job was not completed. Brigadier Croft, 9th (Scottish) Division noted before the division left the area in 1916:

Patrols were sent over into The Birdcage one last time, and found British losses lying out in No-Man's Land! They had been there over a year, but because of the enemy alertness, and the impassable marshy ground, it had been impossible to bring them in!

Some of these unfortunates must have been from 19 December 1914 raid on The Birdcage, as there had been no further attempt to force its defences since that raid. A proposal by the German 'Acting General Command' for a formal armistice on 31 December 1914 to collect and bury the dead who had fallen close to and behind the enemy lines had been handed to a Rifle Brigade stretcher-bearer during the Christmas Truce. Nothing came of it as the Rifle Brigade did not have the authority to meet the strict conditions laid down by the proposal which detailed that the Germans would collect the bodies and carry them to British stretcher-parties and that British and German artillery were to hold their fire between 10 am and 2 pm – 'German time' as the proposal stated. The truce was also enjoyed in northern France but there is no evidence to suggest that it took place north of the Messines sector. Both sides welcomed the truce, which in some areas continued through to the New Year, but it was not taken in the same spirit by higher command who issued directives to ensure that such happenings should not happen again.

The road running westward to La Hutte from St. Yves follows along a rise in the ground and passes Prowse Point British Military Cemetery, named after Major C. B. Prowse, 1st Battalion Somerset Light Infantry, for an action he initiated and commanded in October 1914. The Somersets had been relieved by the Hampshire Regiment on 28 October after a stint on the Le Gheer–River Douve front and had retired to the second line trenches north of the wood:

> The 29 October passed quietly for the Somersets, with little action from an enemy who had been attacking continuously to break through in this sector – a lapse in the fighting that was noted with suspicion by battalion command. The most peaceful day for a long time. Fear it might be the calm before the storm

At about 7 am on 30 October, enemy artillery bombarded the trenches all along the area between the River Warnave and the River Douve and continued to do so until mid-afternoon. About midday, word was received from St. Yves that the Germans were massing in force in front of the Hampshires' trenches. The situation there was becoming critical with the German infantry only 300 yards from the Hampshires who had already lost a platoon and a section of its trenches in a sunken road just before the rise where today sits Prowse Point Military Cemetery. A company of Somersets commanded by Second Lieutenant A. V. Braithwaite was sent to reinforce the Hampshires, arriving just as the enemy were pouring through the line where the platoon had been annihilated. The Somersets hastily erected a barricade from behind which they took heavy toll of the attackers, who continued to amass in the trench, relentlessly attacking the barricade in a bid to break through and move on. Another company of Somersets was dispatched as further reinforcements for a situation that was becoming more desperate by the minute. A breakthrough would have serious consequences for British positions further south and battalion headquarters, in an estaminet at Hyde Park Corner, a road junction near the north-west corner of the wood, realised that this break in the line needed more than a barricade to reinstate the British front.

At 5.30 pm Major Prowse, then battalion commander, himself reconnoitred the position and found the Germans not only occupying the trench taken from the Hampshires but holding buildings in the vicinity as well. He decided to counter-attack that night, his plan being to move forward without a supporting barrage, surround the trench and the buildings and attack and clear them at the point of the bayonet. He led the attack himself, with two companies armed only with small arms and bayonets. The speed and ferocity of this attack quickly overcame the enemy who rapidly vacated the area. The Somersets incurred no casualties during the action resulting in a 'Bloodless Victory' (for them that is) and, for his initiative and leadership in this action Major Prowse was promoted to Lieutenant Colonel and awarded the Distinguished Service Order.

Prowse Farm on the Frezenberg Ridge was also named after him for his activities there in 1915. He was promoted to Brigadier General in 1916 taking command of the 11th Brigade, 4th Division. Wounded near th Quadrilateral, Serre (Somme), on 1 July, he died the next day and was buried Vachelles before being moved to the British Military Cemetery at Louvencourt.

Second Lieutenant A. V. Braithwaite, 'The Hero of the Barricades' as the Somersets christened him, was awarded the Military Cross and mentioned in despatches and his NCO, Sergeant C. Wilcox, received the Distinguished Conduct Medal for gallantry at the barricade. Braithwaite was later killed at the Quadrilateral Redoubt. His name is on the Thiepval British Memorial to the

Prowse Point Cemetery from Mud Corner.

Missing and a family memorial stands on the site of his death beside the Serre Road Cemetery No. 2, Beaumont Hamel (Somme).

South of Prowse Point, the view embraces the gentle slope down to the brooding mass of the wood which cloaks the approaches to Armentières. It was up this slope that Major Prowse and the Somersets moved forward to ease the pressure on their beleaguered colleagues and to rout a determined enemy.

The small track running down the slope from here was called Mud Lane, finding its way along to Hyde Park Corner on the Armentières–Messines road, a main route for troops moving into the front-line from that area. At the bottom of the slope, where it bears right to follow the northern edge of the wood, is Mud Corner, today the name of the military cemetery sited there. This corner is the official entry to the wood and the three military cemeteries within. In the winter months, the low-lying section of Mud Lane from Mud Corner to Hyde Park Corner fully justifies its name, given to it by the legions of laden men who passed this way before the corduroy track was in general use.

Further down the lane, Lieutenant R. B. Talbot Kelly, serving here in 1917 as a Forward Observation Officer, recalls:

> My section had a forward gun on the edge of the wood near Mud Lane. The pit lay in a verdant thicket of little willows and blackberry bushes. Ten yards away, a wooden cross marked the grave of Ronnie Poulton (sic), prince of rugger players, whom, as a boy at school, I had often seen run through a complete team to score a dazzling try. I felt here was a strange re-union of Rugbeians, dead and living in a glade in Arcady!

Moated Farm in December 1914.

He was looking at the Royal Berkshires' regimental burial plot where Lieutenant Ronald Poulton Palmer the England and Harlequin rugby captain had been buried. This burial plot was then on the corner of the crossroads where Mud Lane met the main road. Today, these crossroads no longer exist as Mud Lane was redirected in the post-war years to meet the main road a little to the north of its original position.

To the left of Mud Corner is Moated Farm which, in early 1916, was manned by the 11th Battalion Royal Scots, 9th (Scottish) Division. On 13 May of that year, the Germans, forever raiding sites around the perimeter of the wood, targeted the farm and its surrounding trenches with a view to destroying a mineshaft they believed to be there. A mine was being run under the trenches in front of those of the Royal Scots and men of the battalion had spent much time in working parties helping the tunnelling company to drive this mine to The Birdcage, close by their positions. The Germans, the 104th Saxons, attacked in three raiding-parties of 20 men each, following a violent barrage of heavy shells and trench mortars. Talbot Kelly takes up the tale again:

> Between St. Yves and the wood, in a little hollow just behind our front lay Moated Farm, a fortified ruin with ten feet of water all round it. It was one of a series of rallying points in case of a successful enemy assault on our front lines. One evening, a violent trench mortar and howitzer bombardment fell upon the farm, and trenches immediately in front of it. From St. Yves, I watched the red dust whirl in eddies around the trees, while the shattering crashes of mortars battered the dusk. The little garrison of Royal Scots were completely cut-off from outside assistance. About dusk it stopped, and reinforcements were rushed up.

The Royal Scots counter-attacked, fighting like "tiger-cats" to quote one account, and drove the Germans back to their own side of the wire. The barrage had accounted for losses to the Royal Scots of 16 killed, 61 wounded and eight missing, and the Germans left behind 10 dead bodies. One man was to benefit well from this raid. Part of the trench line that had taken a major part of the bombardment with all the men being killed except for one officer and a private who was serving a three-year sentence in the line for attempted desertion. During the raid he bayoneted and killed six Germans while the officer killed two with his revolver, obviously taking seriously the GOC 9th Division's directive that men in the line should treat their area, No-Man's Land included, as "Ninth Division Land" and that "corpses are more important than acres". The raiders then decided to beat a hasty retreat. For this effort the officer won the Military Cross and the private had his sentence quashed.

To the north of Prowse Point, perched on the skyline of the ridge, is the Messines church. A familiar sight to British troops, although then a more battered and menacing one than today, with the slopes of the ridge scarred with tiers of trenches peering into their positions. It was a constant reminder of the men who occupied the village and the ridge named after it, giving them such superior observation all along the front from Plugstreet to Hill 60 in the north.

Directly north and opposite Prowse Point, on a line between it and the church, sits Anton's Farm, an important British fortified farmhouse right on the British front-line named after, like so many fortified farms, the Royal Engineer responsible for much of its structure. To the east of this farm, either side of what was called Anton's Farm Road, two mine craters mark the spot of another German strongpoint which went the way of its brethren on the outset of the Messines Offensive. The 171st Tunnelling Company, working from Trench 127, duly completed the shaft but, with the drive well on its way to its destination, about 700 feet from its beginning at the shaft-base, the top left-hand corner of the drive collapsed and 35 feet of it was quickly filled with quicksand, causing not a little concern, and a great deal of inconvenience, to the men working there. A temporary sandbag dam was built immediately and then a concrete dam, backed by a 30-foot wall of sandbags and then another concrete dam, and all this at 70 feet below the ground. A new drive was started, running beneath the collapsed section. At 761 feet from the drive entrance, and now 90 feet below the surface, a branch gallery was dug leading left, running on another 200 feet where the chamber was finally completed and charged with 36,000 lbs of ammonal. The main drive was continued to 1,357 feet, chambered and charged with 50,000 lbs of ammonal.

The two craters tranquil now in their position astride Anton's Farm Road are the results of all that work. What happened to those two concrete dams embracing a 30-foot wall of sandbags? Who knows? They may well still be intact, waiting to be discovered by a future generation of deep-digging Belgians who will surely wonder how this strange artefact got there in the first place.

Anton's Farm from Prowse Point, with the Messines church on the skyline. The field in front is the turnip field where Bairnsfather recorded the Christmas Truce of 1914.

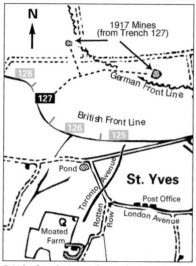

N
1917 Mines
(from Trench 127)

128
127
German Front Line
British Front Line
126
125
Pond
St. Yves
Toronto Avenue
Post Office
London Avenue
Rotten Row
Moated Farm

British front-line trench numbering showing Trench 127 and the mine-craters either side of Anton's Farm road.

Just after midnight on the morning of 5 May, 1915, Lieutenant Ronald Poulton Palmer of the 1/4th Royal Berkshire Regiment was sniped while supervising a company working-party detailed for dugout repair in the trenches straddling Anton's Farm.

Lieutenant Poulton Palmer of the Huntley & Palmer biscuit company family, was a great uncle of Virginia Bottomley, former British Cabinet Minister and M.P. A famous rugby player, he captained his county and England as well as being a member of the Harlequins Club. His last game for England was against France at Parc des Princes in July 1914. His final game of rugby was as captain of a 48th Division team against the 4th Division at Pont de Nieppe on 14 April 1915. At the time, there were those who felt that his death was not an accident of war, more a premeditated killing of a well-known and much admired public figure, intended to demoralise his fellow soldiers as well as the British public. At his death, his men were seen crying in the trenches and many of them kept a photograph of him pinned to the trench walls. His body was carried to a field ambulance at the nunnery (referred to as an hospice by Churchill) on the Le Bizet road at Plugstreet and buried in the regimental plot at Hyde Park Corner at 6.30 pm on the evening of 6 May, the Bishop of Pretoria presiding over the ceremony. At the time of his burial there was only one other grave in the cemetery, that of Private Frederick W. Giles who had been sniped the previous month, 28 April, and had actually fallen, wounded, on Poulton Palmer when he was shot. He died the same day.

Lieutenant Poulton Palmer, 1/4th Battalion, Royal Berkshire Regiment.

The first officer in his battalion to fall, Poulton Palmer was a great loss to his fellow officers, his battalion, his sport and to the shocked public of his country. Many men of the battalion wrote letters home telling of their deep admiration for him, an extract from one of them giving a good indication of how the men felt:

He was our most popular officer and everybody loved him, and when our turn comes to charge the Germans we shall do so with the name of Palmer on our lips.

Ronald Poulton Palmer's grave marker at the Hyde Park Corner (Royal Berks) Cemetery, 1915.

A newspaper article echoed similar sentiments in a quote from an NCO who contributed to the article:

He was the finest and best loved officer in the whole Brigade, and I pity the Germans who run across his Company when there is an attack.

Further proof of his popularity is supported by the number of mentions made to the sighting of his grave in divisional, brigade and battalion histories and personal memoirs of the war.

North of Anton's Farm, another farm sits just south of the River Douve. La Douve Farm, one of three farms taking their names from the river, came into prominence on 1 November 1914 when the 2nd Royal Inniskilling Fusiliers destroyed a tactical advance of the Germans attempting to move on to the Channel Ports. After its successful part in the action at Le Gheer crossroads on 21 October, the 2nd Battalion were billeted in Plugstreet acting as brigade reserve. They were back in the line again on 31 October, successfully retaking trenches north of the River Douve from which a garrison of the 57th Rifles, Lahore Division attached to the 1st Cavalry Division, had been driven out, leaving the Cavalry Division holding this sector of the line, in an open-flanked position. After restoring this line, the Inniskillings were called on to fill a gap on the left flank of the 4th Division.

Poulton Palmer's grave marker today, inset into the eastern wall of Holywell Cemetery, Oxford.

High Command eventually decided that the position was not important enough to maintain and called for a withdrawal to its second line in front of Hill 63 and the Armentières–Messines road. The 4th Division withdrew to lines south of the River Douve where the Royal Inniskillings were instructed to hold the left flank running parallel to the river. The order never reached two companies of the battalion and they settled down for the night, unaware that they were on their own. The next day, 1 November the Kaiser briefly stated:

By order of His Majesty the Kaiser, Douve Farm is to be stormed today!

... and it was, giving two Inniskilling companies a field day. With an enemy advancing in strength, in the open, only 150 yards away, the Inniskillings held a turkey-shoot. Consistent and rapid fire smashed the German advance, inflicting heavy losses on a surprised, but dutifully advancing attack force. The Germans eventually succeeded in occupying the farm, mainly because British Command decided that the trench lines in the area were untenable, and only after those two companies of the Inniskillings had frustrated the Kaiser himself by hindering part of his personally directed strategic plan. A report in the battalion diary describes the action as:

Men of the Royal Berks Regiment sniping from the roof of Anton's Farm.

All day we saw the enemy massed on the ridge and advancing toward our line. I decided that we must endeavour to deceive them as to our strength and having a good supply of S.A.A. bursts of rapid fire were kept up throughout the day. The rifles of casualties also being used. I think the enemy were uncertain as to our position - I know they had many casualties and did not press their attack that day ... Under cover of darkness we collected our casualties and withdrew.

The Official History of the War, Military Operations, France and Belgium, 1914-1918, noted that the result of this happy accident of poor communication to the two Royal Inniskilling companies had: " ... achieved a decided triumph."

La Douve Farm was not rebuilt but a farm just south of it, Avenue Farm then, today carries its name. Due west of it, on the left hand side of the Armentières–Messines road as it mounts the slope at the base of the Messines Ridge sits a large farm. La Petite Douve Farm, the second of the three Douve farms, held a position immediately on the German firing line just north of the little bridge carrying the road across the river. The Germans transformed this one into a strongpoint named *Weihauchtshof* (Christmas Court in English), a dominant position commanding excellent observation over the ground which any Allied attack from the direction of northern France would need to cover.

In October 1915, the Canadians were serving in this area and, until then, a live-and-let-live attitude existed on both sides of the line. The 2nd Infantry Brigade, 1st Canadian Division, decided to change all that, and the German 11th Reserve Infantry Regiment in the farm at the time were due for a rude

What remained of La Douve Farm in 1917.

awakening. 'Passive defence', as far as the British Army, and particularly the Canadians, were concerned, was deemed a thing of the past and that the forthcoming winter would be spent in hard training in anticipation of future operations. Short, heavy bombardments would keep the enemy in a constant state of alert, sniping was to be developed to a fine art, and trench raiding, introduced the previous summer, would be a regular activity.

A raid was planned for the Canadian 7th Battalion (British Columbia) and 5th Battalion (Saskatchewan), 2nd Infantry Brigade, on 17 November. Their target, the front-line trenches at La Petite Douve Farm, their objectives: a) to secure prisoners for interrogation; b) to destroy dugouts and capture documents; and c) to persuade the enemy to call up his reserves to man the trenches, thus preparing a first class target for the British bombardment timed to immediately follow the raid.

The German line north of the River Douve jutted out from the farm in a salient over 500 yards in length before crossing the Armentières–Messines road. The section along the edge of the road from the farm to the bridge where the main road crossed the river was the 7th Battalion's target, supported by a diversionary attack by the 5th on the fortified La Douve Farm 1,000 yards to the east just behind the German line. Aggressive patrolling in the days before the raid caused the resident garrison to withdraw its screen of sentry and listening posts. The day prior to the raid, British and Canadian 18-pounders and trench mortars pummelled the farm and the raiding parties moved into their jumping-off positions. They had removed all identification and donned black crêpe masks,

The River Douve winding its way from the Messines road to La Douve Farm, rebuilt just south of its original moated position on the site of another farm named Avenue Farm during the war.

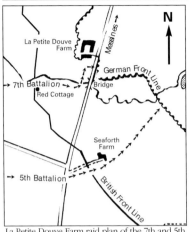

La Petite Douve Farm raid plan of the 7th and 5th Battalions, 2nd Canadian Infantry Brigade at 2.30 am on 17 November 1915.

primarily as camouflage but also to present a ghoulish presence which, coupled with the surprise of the attack, would add a terrifying aspect for the enemy. The masks were also a form of identification - anyone without a black face was a target for extinction. At 2.30 am on 17 November, both raiding parties set out towards the enemy lines, in parallel but separated by about 500 yards. Almost immediately, the 5th Battalion raiders encountered a bank of German wire along a ditch. The leading men became entangled and struggled to disengage themselves, the enemy opened fire and, short of their objective, the raiders were forced to retaliate and eventually retire.

The 7th Battalion moved quickly to the bridge, scaled the embankment, overcame the enemy's forward posts, sited bombing blocks and wire, and posted sentries on the flanks to repel counter-attacks. They then withdrew, achieving all objectives, having killed or wounding 30 of the enemy. They returned with 12 prisoners of the 2nd Battalion, 11th Prussian Regiment, a great deal of information and, as a bonus for Allied intelligence, a new design of gas mask

La Petite Douve Farm under shell-fire in October 1915.

recently issued by the enemy. The Germans retaliated with a hastily mounted infantry attack which was effectively stopped by Allied artillery. Private J. Mead of the 7th Battalion, snagged his rifle on the wire and was shot while struggling to free himself. He was buried by the river but the grave was lost in later fighting. His name is on the Menin Gate Memorial at Ypres. Lieutenant H. Owen, the architect of the raid was killed in January 1916 on another raid and buried in the 2nd Canadian Infantry Brigade plot at Rosenberg Château. The raid was a great success and the Canadians became adept at this sort of activity and showed their prowess many times, in many places through the long war years to come. The enemy reaction to this particular skill of the Canadians is well covered in a diary taken from a German captured on the Somme. An entry noted:

> It is a relief to get from the trenches opposing those verdammte 'Canadian redskins'. They are terrible, and fight without any rules whatsoever. One never knows what they may do.

Several weeks later, at the same bridge, the 5th Battalion were in action again, but this time with more success than they earned on 17 November. In the summer months, troops occupying trenches west of the Armentières–Messines road and due south of La Petite Douve Farm reported evidence of mine workings. Listening posts were strengthened and patrols investigated the area but to no avail, nevertheless, the subject of German underground operations continued to be discussed by various commands in the area. In early December, patrols of the 2nd Canadian Mounted Rifles discovered a strong enemy-constructed barrier across the road just north of the bridge and orders

The road to Messines in November 1914. The house to the left was the lodge at the entrance to Château de la Hutte, the approximate spot from which the Canadians manhandled their gun to its position in front of La Petite Douve Farm to destroy the barricade on 15 December 1915.

were issued for its immediate destruction. A Canadian attack was set up for 4 December but proved abortive. Another on 8-9 December by men of Lord Strathcona's Horse was also unsuccessful, with the attackers taking 11 casualties. Then the 5th Battalion volunteered to do something about it and devised a plan that was successfully carried out on the morning of 15 December.

Short bombardments were put down in the afternoons and during the nights of 12, 13 and 14 December and a shorter one at 4 am on 15th – this was the one that determined the outcome of the raid. On the 13th, the defenders had been driven out of the barricade by shell-fire and fled for cover. Six were quickly accounted for, five by Sergeant J. S. McGlashan of the 5th Battalion. On the night of 14-15th, the 3rd Battery Canadian Field Artillery placed an 18-pounder in the front-line directly opposite the barricade. It had been towed up the Armentières–Messines road to Château de la Hutte by an armoured car from where it was manhandled into position so as not to allow the sound of the motor to be heard by the enemy. The attack parties removed all badges and numerals from their tunics, blackened their faces and hands with charcoal and the bayonet men fixed flashlights to their rifles. The flanking parties then slid over the parapet and crouched to the left and right of the road. At 4 am the gun fired three rounds of heavy explosive and 22 rounds of shrapnel at point blank range, and that was the end of the German barricade. At 4.05 am, the attackers rushed the position to find only two defenders still alive. These they took back to the Canadian line together with seven rifles and a bag of bombs, having first mined the position against further occupation. The operation had been a complete success with only two Canadians receiving minor wounds.

La Petite Douve Farm north of the bridge spanning the River Douve. The road to Messines is to the farm's right with the distinctive tower of the church of Messines visible on the skyline. It was immediately north of this bridge that the Germans built their barricade in 1915.

The two prisoners were of the 3rd Battalion 11th Reserve Infantry Regiment, 117th Division. Under interrogation, they stated that their company, the 12th, had replaced the 5th Company 2nd Battalion, which had been withdrawn in disgrace following the Canadian raid on 17 November.

The barricade obliterated and the raid over, the gun now had to be removed from the front-line. It was decided that the armoured car should be run up to the line, regardless of risk, to retrieve it. Within 200-yards of the front trench, the car became ditched in a road cave-in. The driver ran down to the front-line trench to get the gun crew to help him pull it out. Another armoured car was called for while the gunners and the driver struggled to extricate the ditched one. The second car arrived but didn't get as far as the first, collapsing through the planked bridge spanning the reserve trench it had to cross. In the meantime, the first car had been dragged out of its hole, backed-up to the front-line trench, hooked up to the gun and was on its way back to safety beyond the reserve trenches only to find the road blocked by the second car. The gun was unhooked from the number one car which then hauled out the number two car from the reserve trench, then re-hooked the gun and sped back to the safety of Hyde Park Corner with number two car in hot pursuit. Thus the episode of La Petite Douve Farm barricade came to a close.

Nothing of much importance happened in or around the area of the farm after the Canadian activities in 1915 and it was eventually taken by the New Zealand Division of Anzac II Corps during the Messines Offensive in 1917. It had been destined to be a target for the mining activities for the attack on the Messines Ridge in 1917, but when the Germans discovered and entered the mine workings, the British decided to abandon it. It's shaft was started by the 3rd Canadian Tunnelling Company from Trench 135 in March 1916, just north-west of the farm. The 171st Tunnelling Company took over the job and, during August, the mine chamber and its charges were completed. The Germans had been running a gallery of their own, virtually alongside that of the British, and were soon aware of what was happening so close to them. They exploded a camouflet in the British gallery destroying about 400 feet of it, and killing four of the men working there. It was so badly damaged, and considered beyond repair, that it was decided that the mine was to be

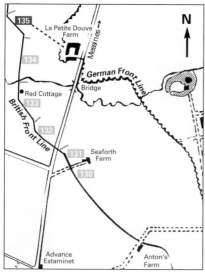

Trench 135 from where the mine below La Petite Douve Farm was driven.

abandoned and the gallery flooded. Having carried out the flooding, the British noticed that he water gradually seeped through to the German gallery, causing untold hours of pumping out water for the enemy engineers. The British carefully monitored the German pumping progress by noting the water level in the destroyed gallery and, when they felt it was low enough, they would replenish the volume with water directly from the river. *The Official History of New Zealand's Effort in the Great War, Vol II, France* recounts:

> The Brits had allowed the Douve to flood their shaft at this point but maintained activity underground in careful scouting of German progress which they anticipated would break into their own abandoned shaft. On 10th January 1917, the water in the British shaft dropped 70 to 80 feet and must have flooded the German galleries. The Germans undertook the fruitless task of pumping out their galleries before realising they were vainly pumping the running water of the Douve.

So ended mining activities in the area of La Petite Douve Farm, the only location where British mine operations supporting the Battle of Messines were destroyed by enemy activity. When the British decided to flood the gallery there is no evidence to suggest they made any effort to remove the mine charges. Because of the gallery's proximity to the River Douve, the charges were packed in water tight tins and, if this method of protection was successful, and there is no reason to suggest it wasn't, then it is fair to say that the charges, 1,500 lbs of ammonal, are still sitting 80-feet below the farm, waiting for the triggering that never came. The shaft from where the Germans started their gallery is still in the farm grounds, its entrance covered by a concrete slab. Should something trigger the mines, that concrete slab could well accompany the farmstead to the destiny intended for it in the original offensive plan for 1917!

South of the farm the road leads to the lower slopes of Hill 63 and down, into the cover afforded by Plugstreet Wood, and then to Ploegsteert village. This part of the sector always saw a great deal of activity with men and transport moving from the back areas to replenish dumps and stores; companies moving in and out of the wood forming reliefs for the trenches east of it, or moving back into reserve after being relieved of trench duty; ambulances and stretcher-parties moving the wounded to the dressing stations behind the hill and further south and west into the back areas and, of course the burial parties carrying out their sad duties in the various burial plots along the way.

It was particularly busy on the evening of 6 June 1917 when two Australian attack battalions made their way along the road to Messines to swing over the top of the wood moving north on to their particular assembly positions south of the River Douve from just below La Petite Douve Farm (destined to be the prize of the New Zealand Division in the forthcoming battle)) to St Yves. They were to launch there attack from this sector the next morning when the explosion of the two Anton's Road mines opened the way for their part in the Battle of Messines.

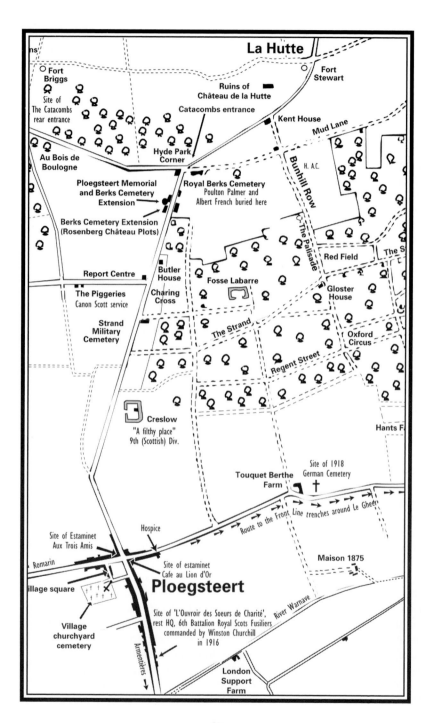

La Hutte

○ Fort Briggs

Fort Stewart ○

Site of The Catacombs rear entrance

Ruins of Château de la Hutte

Catacombs entrance

Kent House

Mud Lane

Au Bois de Boulogne

Hyde Park Corner

Ploegsteert Memorial and Berks Cemetery Extension

Royal Berks Cemetery
Poulton Palmer and Albert French buried here

H. A.C.

Bunhill Row

Berks Cemetery Extension (Rosenberg Château Plots)

The Palisade

Red Field

The S

Report Centre

Butler House

Fosse Labarre

The Piggeries
Canon Scott service

Charing Cross

Gloster House

Strand Military Cemetery

The Strand

Oxford Circus

Regent Street

Creslow
"A filthy place"
9th (Scottish) Div.

Hants F

Site of 1918 German Cemetery

Touquet Berthe Farm

Route to the Front Line trenches around Le Gheer

Hospice

Maison 1875

Site of Estaminet Aux Trois Amis

Romarin

Site of estaminet Cafe au Lion d'Or

Village square

Ploegsteert

River Warnave

Village churchyard cemetery

Site of 'L'Ouvroir des Soeurs de Charité', rest HQ, 6th Battalion Royal Scots Fusiliers commanded by Winston Churchill in 1916

Armentières

London Support Farm

CHAPTER 4

LA HUTTE TO PLUGSTREET

S OUTHWEST OF LA PETITE DOUVE FARM is another one of the many hamlets
scattered over this sector of southern Belgium. This particular one, Le
Rossignol, gives its name to Rossignol Hill, the 63-metre high knoll which
became the Hill 63 of the British Army. During the war, the hill was smothered
with redoubts, trenches, machine-gun posts, observation posts and gun-
emplacements. It commanded views of Mont Kemmel and Mont des Cats to
the west and enjoyed extensive views eastward, down the valley of the River
Douve and along the German-occupied southern slopes of the Messines Ridge
to Warneton and its distinctive water-tower (referred to by the troops as
Warneton Tower).

The hill was well known by locals because of the two châteaux it boasted.
The one high on the eastern slope, Château de la Hutte, (known as Hennessy's
Château by the troops but it was never owned by that family), embraced the
hill and Plugstreet Wood itself within its estate. The château was used by
General de Lisle as the headquarters of the 1st Cavalry Brigade in November
1914 but was abandoned after the General's chauffeur was killed and his car
destroyed during a bout of enemy gunfire. It was quickly and efficiently
destroyed by German guns early in the war because of its presence so close to
their lines and its obvious potential of providing a superb observation post for
the artillery. As it was, its destruction did not affect its use for observation purpose, nor its cellars being used as shelters for the artillerymen manning the guns
in their emplacements in the château grounds. It wasn't rebuilt after the war
and today its footings and cellars are now part-covered with grassland and can
barely be seen, but the general condition of the land around its site gives clear
indication of the shell-battering it took during the war years.

The Canadian forces very early in the war quickly came to the conclusion
that the mathematics involved when considering a crew of six men firing a
machine gun at 300 rounds a minute against one man firing a rifle at 15 rounds
a minute leant very much in favour of the former. It had taken British
Headquarters Staff a long time to work this out but, in the meantime, the
Canadians had formed the 1st Canadian Motor Machine Gun Brigade, later
abbreviated to the 1st Motors. In September 1915 the 1st Motors had set up in

Château de La Hutte before the war.

The ruins of Château de la Hutte in 1915.

the stables of the Château de la Hutte and were using the château cellars as billets. One day a sergeant discovered, hidden behind a pile of bricks and rubble in a corner of the cellars, a locked door behind which a staircase led down to a sub-cellar where, behind another locked door, lay the greater part of the château's stock of wine. This was soon distributed among the officers and men, with dozens of bottles being buried carefully and safely in a reinforced pit in the château gardens. Even after this share out there was a considerable amount of stock remaining, so it was decided to offer the surplus to the divisional commander, General Currie. The General was extremely thankful for the offer but he insisted on sharing the wine with the officers of the 1st Motors. For the sake of good manners, and to save the General, and themselves, embarrassment, they chose not to tell him that their mess stock, and that of the men, was already full to capacity, so they 'reluctantly' accepted his offer.

A captain in the Argyll and Sutherland Highlanders returning to the sector in 1915, having served there the previous year, remembered the days he used to get champagne out of the cellars of the château. He rued the day when the château was reduced to the ruin he saw in 1915. Had he known that men of the Canadian 1st Motors later in the year had discovered a horde of wine in the sub-cellars of the château he may well have rued the day he did not search for more than champagne when given the chance. Later in the year he would have noted that the ruins had been reduced to a heap of rubble, indirectly caused by the same Canadians who discovered the wine.

The pile of rubble in late 1915 that was once the Château de la Hutte.

During their stay at the château senior officers of the Canadian 1st Motors, had noted a spot about 500 yards behind the enemy lines where German artillery officers congregated at the same hour daily. The Canadians arranged for their machine-guns to disturb this gathering a number of times before the

Rosenberg Château in as it was when British troops first arrived in the sector.

German artillery officers took offense and called up an 8-inch naval gun and fired ten rounds into the ruins of the château. There were no casualties, the machine-gunners being in the stables, the wine safely in its pit, but the already battered château was reduced to a heap of rubble.

The hill's steep southern slopes were scattered with log huts and cabins used as billets for battalions supporting the front-line troops. Amongst these log 'dwellings' sat the more substantially built Rosenberg Château, damaged by enemy gunfire at the beginning of the conflict in this area. Its lodge house sits at the entrance to the château driveway on the road, then called Red Lodge Road leading from Hyde Park Corner and the Armentières–Messines road and on towards the hamlet of Romarin and the village of Neuve Eglise. This lodge, together with a farm to the left of it, Underhill Farm and the château itself, were collectively called Red Lodge during the war, the red brickwork of the lodge house being the reason behind the name. The Red Lodge complex was used as a billeting area and dressing stations by units stationed in the area and, as with all such stations, they soon featured the sad sights of burial plots nearby. The New Zealand units were to use Underhill Farm as their Central Dressing

The fire-damaged Rosenberg Château in late 1914. It was later reduced to rubble by both German and British gunfire, the British needing the bricks to use as horse standings and for other 'war-like' purposes.

Station to support their action at the Battle of Messines in 1917. The farm plot was referred to as "the military cemetery at the foot of Nightingale Hill" by the Germans who used it in early 1918, 'Nightingale' being the German and English translation of the French 'Rossignol'. In the post-war years the farm, with its cemetery nestling alongside, was rebuilt on its original site but the château was rebuilt closer to the road that runs up the hill from a turning just west of the cemetery. Its lodge house still guards the entrance to the château grounds but this entrance is no longer used as an access for the château.

The 'Red Lodge' at the entrance of Rosenberg Château driveway, November 1914. In 1917 the Catacomb's side-entrances and report-centre was situated just by the general-purpose wagon in front of the limbers.

'Red Lodge' today.

Early in the war, two burial plots were started in the château grounds under the names Rosenberg Château and Extension. In 1930 the War Graves Commission, well into their task of recording the dead and gathering graves together into the official military cemeteries, were asked to close these plots and move the bodies to another cemetery. The owner of the château had decided to rebuild it as his family home and had refused to allow the British fallen to rest within his estate. By virtue of an agreement signed at Le Havre on 9 August 1917, the Belgian government had undertaken to acquire properties containing the burial plots from their owners in order that construction of permanent cemeteries could take place. The owner's resistance to the Le Havre agreement caused concern at meetings of the Anglo-Belgium Committee in Brussels, and the matter developed into an emotive issue between the two former allies. The Belgian Minister of the Interior intervened when questions were raised in the respective parliaments and letters appeared in the national press of both nations. However, the Minister, whose position corresponded with that of the British Home Secretary, had no power to coerce the owner of Rosenberg Château who was acting fully within his rights. To have fought the matter through the Belgian courts would have meant certain and humiliating defeat for the British Government, so it took the only course available to it and arranged to move the bodies to another cemetery. Consequently 477 men from the United Kingdom, Canada, Australia and New Zealand were exhumed and, with full military honours, laid to rest in a specially designated section,

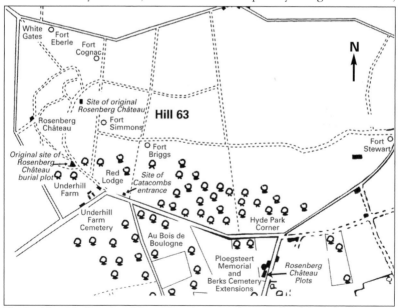

The site of the original Rosenberg Château Military Cemetery and Extension burial plots before the removal of the graves in 1931 to Hyde Park Corner.

Rosenberg Château Plots, south of the Berks Cemetery Extension at Hyde Park Corner. Today the Ploegsteert Memorial is sited between these two cemeteries.

Just along the road, Red Lodge Road, leading back from the lodge to Hyde Park Corner is the site of some of the entrances to what must have been one of the most ambitious workings attempted by the military during the war on either side. It lay in the lee of the hill, making it quite impervious to all but the most unlucky of shelling. Constructed over a period of only three months by

Men of the Australian 6th Brigade lining Plumer Road at the entrance to Wallangara, or The Catacombs as it was generally called.

the 1st Australian Tunnelling Company, it was used by many Australians and other units during the years 1917 and 1918. Officially called Hill 63 Dugouts, the Australians gave it the picturesque name of Wallangara, although it was more generally called 'The Catacombs', but affectionately known as "The Hole in the Hill", by many Australian troops. The system of chambers with connecting galleries, entrances and exits had bunk sleeping accommodation for 1,200 men within and for a further 250 officers and men in steel-huts outside, the latter being covered with spoil from the workings. There were nineteen 'streets' within, lined with bunks, with some of the 'streets' sectioned off for officers and their batmen. Senior officer quarters were set up as 'rooms' with two bunks and a table, whereas platoon officers were housed in similar but smaller rooms without a table. Thirty-eight bunks were set aside for runners and clerks close to a large General Office and Signals Office It also housed electrical units for electric lighting and signal equipment, a canteen and a small hospital. This 'Hole in the Hill' had three exits to the south and three to the north. The main entrance at Hyde Park Corner was large enough to allow a large sized wagon to enter, and was configured in two one-way passage systems to enable the entering and leaving of hundreds of men to be conducted in an orderly manner. Almost every unit passing to and fro in the area spent a night in the "The Catacombs of Hill 63". The construction, cut deep into the hillside, was ambitious enough in itself, but the opening ceremony in the spring of 1917 far exceeded any other occasion of importance that had taken place so close to the front-line. Given the honour of opening The Catacombs was the 2nd Army Commander, General Plumer, accompanied by an entourage of nineteen generals and their staffs. The entrance was covered by an archway of tree branches and dressed-overall with coloured bunting. A regimental band was in atten-

Spoil from the Catacombs below Hill 63.

dance and the crowd of onlookers was added-to by officers and men from neighbouring billets. A traffic jam developed in the road as drivers of passing transports abandoned their vehicles and jostled in the crowd determined not to miss anything, curious to know why so many 'Red Tabs' were in evidence. The ceremony finished without any interruption from an enemy who, had he known what was happening, with a few well placed high explosive or shrap-

A pencil sketch drawn by C. M. Sheldon in early 1918, before the German spring offensive of that year showing 'The Hole in the Hill'. It appeared in *War Illustrated* on 8 June 1918.

nel salvoes could well have dramatically changed the thinking, the roster and the future movement of British High Command for the rest of the war. After the ceremony had finished and the dignitaries had returned to places far behind the front, the Australian troops sign-posted the entrance path into their shelters as Plumer Road. Whether or not this was a compliment to General Plumer, or just a gesture reflecting the Aussie sense of humour regarding his surname (pronouncing it as 'Plumber) was never recorded. Today the many entrances and exits to these workings are filled-in and are well covered by the natural growth of the wood, but the actual sites of three access points from the road are identified by what appears to be concrete 'bridges' or culverts, three of them spanning the ditch that runs along the side of the road. Level with one of them, just within the wood, is a concrete shelter of the guard office or report centre type. This could have been the main entrance for transports and supplies to report in or register before moving in to one of the three southerly access points, or maybe the 'bridges' identify the paths to the three southerly entrances themselves. The main entrance and exit for troops was at the corner of Hyde Park Corner where Red Lodge Road meets the Armentières–Messines road. Further within the wood passing left and right of the report centre, is a large area of unnatural groups of tree-covered mounds. Similar mounds are in evidence all along the tree line edging the area embracing the three 'bridges' and stretching along Red Lodge Road. These mounds could well be covering the extra dugouts and shelters made up with the 'spoil' from the main digging within the hill. but otherwise there is little evidence to mark the place as one of the most enterprising examples of battlefield architecture from the Great War. Although

The entrance to The Catacombs in the 1920s.

An aeriel view of Hill 63, the Catacombs and the village of Ploegsteert in 1918 (Photograph courtesy of Paul Reed, Somme, France).

there is evidence of collapse on the slopes above the underground billets, an initiative by the owners of the wood and the authorities could part recover The Catacombs and position this area of the old Western Front as having a battle-field artefact every bit as interesting as that of the Canadian Grange Tunnel at Vimy in France.

Red Lodge Road was always busy during the war years with transports, ambulances, ration and ammunition parties and a host of other groups of men going about their duties, hidden from the ever-searching eyes of the enemy by the heights of Hill 63 and the mass of Plugstreet Wood. It was used mainly to

The communication trench leading from Red Lodge Road near Hyde Park Corner to the summit of Hill 63.

A trench line on the summit of Hill 63 in 1919.

service regimental headquarters, stores, aid posts and other safe dugout areas. A communication trench at the Hyde Park Corner end of it climbed the side of the hill to the many observation-posts on its summit. This trench, as with others on the slopes and on the crest of the hill, didn't suffer the penalties of those in the often boggy, marshy lowlands of the area - the need to add breastworks, rebuild collapsing walls or continually replace sunken or damaged duckboard being alien to trenches on the higher ground. It was free of natural wear-and-tear caused by the non-stop traffic of columns of men, and did not incur the regular damage caused by gunfire as did the front-line, support, reserve and communication trenches on the more exposed areas of the lower ground. Used exclusively by the gunners and others who needed to visit and use the gun batteries and observation posts, it did have the disadvantage of turning into a fast-running river during the rainy season. This problem was overcome by:

... a wonderfully-made trench with a duckboard raised high above the flood of rain and revetted with corrugated iron, reflecting sweating heat as you toiled up.

Men from the hutted camps in the Romarin area would make their way to positions on top of the hill, or to Ration Farm and La Plus Douve Farm (the third of the Douve-named farms) further north, by taking the road turning off Red Lodge Road by Underhill Farm, past the hillside shrine and White Gates (named after the gates of the western entrance of Rosenberg Château).

From positions at Ration Farm and La Plus Douve Farm, British observers were able to look straight down the valley of the River Douve, keeping their eyes on events at La Petite Douve Farm, just 1,000-yards away. This area, on and behind Hill 63, was dotted with shattered farms used as forts, headquarters, *matériel* dumps and troop mustering points, their names forgotten and their inhabitants long gone from the war zone. They were mostly rechristened with titles that reflected the humour and realism of the soldier and were 'officialised' by their inclusion on trench maps of the time.

Other troops from the camps at Romarin, heading for duties in the main body of the wood, would ignore the turning by Underhill Farm and continue past Red Lodge and The Catacombs and onward to Hyde Park Corner, crossing the main Armentières–Messines road, then on into the wood.

The wooded area south of the stretch of road from Red Lodge to Hyde Park Corner, known as Au Bois de Boulogne, was used extensively to bivouac troops held in reserve for the trench lines in front of Hill 63 and the River Douve to the north. To the right of this wooded area, at Hyde Park Corner itself, are two military cemeteries and the Ploegsteert Memorial to the Missing. One of these, Berks Cemetery Extension, was originally on the other side of the road just north of the Hyde Park Corner (Royal Berks) Cemetery, acting, as its name implies, as an extension to the main Royal Berkshire Regimental plot. It was moved to its current position to the right of Au Bois de Boulogne and developed as a complex in the late 1920s, housing the Ploegsteert Memorial and the Berks Cemetery Extension (Rosenberg Château Plots) just south of it.

The section of the Armentières–Messines road running southward to the crossroads at Ploegsteert village was lined with trenches and dugouts used by working parties and reserve troops. On the corner of the right-turn off the main road just below Hyde Park Corner stood a house the troops named the Report Centre. Once used as a Headquarters' site for various battalions, it started a new life monitoring all entrants to this little road which was, and still is, the only access to a grouping of farm buildings further down on the left called The Piggeries and, at the end of the road, a moated farm called La Grande Munque Farm. The latter was the headquarters of the 1st Canadian Division during the winter of 1915. Its moat, dry in the summer, was often used by the garrison staff for sleeping in. At the war's outset, The Piggeries housed the prize herd belonging to the King of the Belgians. This pig farm, with the main building holding up to 200 men, was completed just before war broke out and was not shown as a feature on any maps – the possibly reason it never suffered serious gunfire. The largest building was furnished with two rows of pigsties in which the men from the many regiments billeted here used to sleep. It was here that Canon Scott, the padre to the Canadian Divisions, was conducting a service one evening having heard that the Canadians billeted there were due back in the trenches before the coming Sunday. He had suggested that a voluntary 'church' service, to be held before their moving into the front line would be a good idea, to which, surprisingly, a large number of the men agreed. At the beginning of the service a fight broke out at the rear of the building and a crowd of the men at the back of the congregation seemed to be more interested in the fight than in the service. Being more than wise to the way of men, Canon Scott thought it better to postpone the service rather than the fight, suggesting that the whole congregation gather at the other end of the hall to watch the fight. This they did and when it was over the service restarted. At the end of it Scott told the men that nothing helped a service as much as the inclusion of a good fight. Today, the only evidence suggesting that anything military, or pugilistic, or holy come to that, was connected with The Piggeries is the concrete sentry box keeping its dignified presence in the yard just inside The Piggeries' entrance.

The Messines–Armentières road down to Ploegsteert village crossroads passes, in a field on its left, a concrete structure with a 'three-humped' earth-roof. The was the Australian 'Charing Cross' Central Advanced Dressing Station, built for the Battle of Messines in 1917. Sited on a clearing called Charing Cross (because, as in London, of its proximity to the entrance of The Strand, a communication trench which ran through the wood), it took over an existing, out-of-use burial plot containing just three graves originating from 1914. After the war this burial plot was known locally as The Australian Cemetery but was renamed Strand Military Cemetery following the concentration of local plots and individual graves by the War Graves Commission. It was in the hands of the Germans from April to September 1918 but, unlike a number of cemeteries in the wood's vicinity, they never used it themselves as a burial plot.

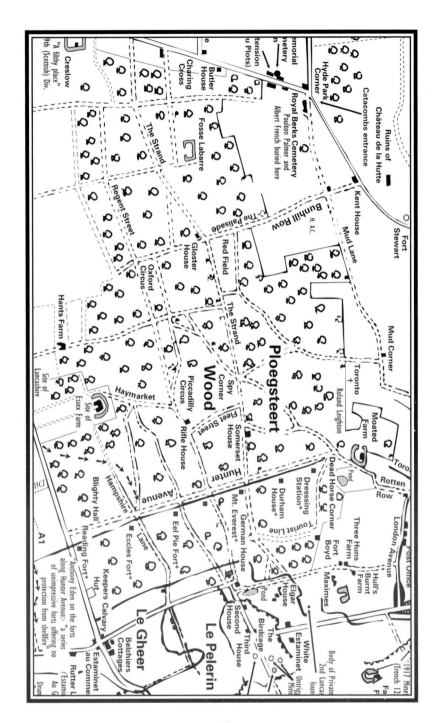

CHAPTER 5

PLUGSTREET WOOD

CHARING CROSS AND THE BEGINNING of The Strand communication trench constituted the main entrance to the wood on its western side. The Strand was a route much used by units and carrying parties on their way to the trench lines during the relatively quiet periods through 1915, '16 and '17. Likewise, it was considered to be the safest route back from the trenches for the wounded to the Armentières-Messines road where they could be collected and transported to the safety of dressing stations around Hill 63 and Ploegsteert village. Although it was called a trench, the major part of its length was a planked road following one of the main rides through the wood. The low ground level at its beginning, not far above sea level, was unsuitable for digging trenches although, as the ground varied in height within the wood, sections of The Strand did take on the guise of a standard trench.

Far into the wood, The Strand bisected Hunter Avenue, a main thoroughfare and fortified line running from the Ploegsteert–Warneton road up to Spy Corner where, swinging to the east, it continued as Rotten Row, on past Moated Farm, entering the curving road of St. Yves at the north-east corner of the wood alongside Bruce Bairnsfather's cottage.

As with farms, buildings and trenches all over the Western Front, the paths, tracks, rides, fire alleys, corners and buildings in and around Plugstreet Wood had been 'officially' named by various regiments serving in the vicinity, and in the case of the wood itself, a preponderance of names with a London connection. Initiated by men of the London Rifle Brigade, who incidentally were responsible for much of the military cartography in the Ploegsteert area at the beginning of the conflict, these reflected the humour and the general, slightly sarcastic attitude of the British soldier to the surroundings he willingly or unwillingly found himself in and, by implication, indicated where he would rather be. It also enabled him to make his mark, letting those who followed know that London regiments had been there first. In many cases, regiments who served in the area at a later date changed the names to suit themselves, – a practice which was not followed by the map makers of the time, causing confusion to readers of battalion diaries and other accounts of actions, but evidently not to the men serving at the time.

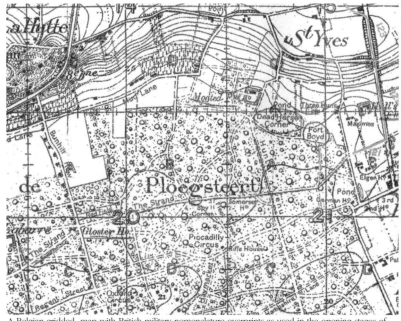

A Belgian gridded map with British military nomenclature overprints as used in the opening stages of the war.

A simplified version of the original Belgian map, the forerunner of the military trench map.

The Strand, Charing Cross, Oxford Circus, Regent Street, Rotten Row, London Avenue, Fleet Street and Hyde Park Corner were examples of the Londoner's desire to walk streets with names he knew, and Bunhill Row clearly identifies the actual regiment which named it, exactly as the London Rifle Brigade, whose headquarters were in Bunhill Row, London, expected it to. All expressed this penchant of the British soldier throughout history to identify places around which he served with names familiar to himself.

Somerset House, Hampshire Lane, Kent House, Gloster House, Hants Farm, Essex Farm, Lancashire Support Farm and Lancashire Cottage are non-London examples of this. Mud Corner and Mud Lane give light to his more descriptive titles for identifying places and routes; Dead Horse Corner where the bones of a long-departed animal hung from a gibbet, served as a landmark rather than a symbol of warning; Blighty Hall needs no explanation – a concrete structured dressing station within the wood, where the wounded were cared for before arrangements would be made to transport them to base hospital, or, hopefully, even to Blighty itself; Rifle House – a timber hut constructed by the 1st Battalion Rifle Brigade as their headquarters; Tourist Line, a reserve trench line running parallel to the northern sector of Hunter Avenue, thought safe enough for visiting dignitaries to visit and to leave, feeling that they had gained experience of front-line warfare; Mount Everest, Eel Pie Fort, with Spy Corner, Moated Farm and many others throughout the wood added to the long list of names – German House and Second and Third House being examples of practicality. The origin of names for others have been lost with the passing of time, although it doesn't stretch the imagination too far to determine why they should be titled so – Maximes, Fort Boyd, Three Huns Farm, Hull's Burnt Farm, White Estaminet, Barricade House etc., and for no apparent reason there were those places that, in the soldier's opinion, did not warrant familiar names – Estaminet au Commerce, Creslow (Creslau on some maps), Touquet Berthe Farm and Fosse Labarre (a narrow horseshoe-shaped ditch or moat enclosing a little garden, which, early in the war was converted into a machine-gun post) for example. Trench maps showing the wood and its surrounds looked more like road maps of a smallish town rather than that of a woodland criss-crossed with rides and fire-alleys.

On arrival in the wood, the British soon set in force a massive programme of constructing a series of concrete forts, log-built huts, dugouts, shelters and breastworks – and of course a network of planked roads, using the wood's fire alleys and rides, to link them all.

The forts, mainly lining the reserve trench line along Hunter Avenue, were small and gave no real protection from direct shelling, but afforded a degree of safety from the shrapnel and small arms fire that ripped through the foliage. The dugouts were seen as resembling: "log-cabins in the backwoods of the Wild West" and those depicted in Bruce Bairnsfather's cartoon drawings were described as:

Royal Engineers building 'roads' in Plugstreet Wood.

Rifle House, headquarters of 1st Battalion Rifle Brigade in Plugstreet Wood, 1914.

... replicas of the little 'bivvies' fashioned out of the breastworks in Plug Street.

The Rifle Brigade originally sited their headquarters in the Report Centre on the corner of the road leading to The Piggeries from the Messines–Armentières road, but later moved to Rifle House within the wood, the log-structured house being built by the machine-gun detachment. It seems that log huts were a speciality of the Rifle Brigade as areas of the wood called Hunston North and Hunston South, both just east of the Messines–Armentières road centred between Plugstreet village and Hyde Park Corner, were turned into a small 'hamlet' by lines of these huts and were used by regiments as headquarters and billets long after the Rifle Brigade had left the area. A description by an officer of the Royal Berkshire Regiment recounts:

Huts were built by the Rifle Brigade at Hunston North in the centre of the wood ... Here we planted a garden around the log-hut which served as a sleeping place and mess, wire bunks in two tiers being arranged round the walls. This was the best camp in the wood, and the safest, though bullets came along occasionally.

Anthony Eden, later a British Prime Minister and future Earl of Avon, serving there with the 21st Battalion King's Royal Rifle Corps in April 1916 described the seven forts alongside Hunter Avenue as:

... a series of unimpressive forts offering no protection from shell fire.

London Rifle Brigade headquarters in Plugstreet Wood 1914.

A. Forestier's impression of a billet in Plugstreet Wood produced for the *Illustrated London News*.

Following the brutal realities of war in the autumn/winter of 1914, and accepting that the war hadn't been won by Christmas, this building operation soon became a point of interest to the British press and articles and drawing began to appear likewise. Plugstreet Wood, because of its 'quiet sector' reputation, began to be used as a form of 'soft' propaganda, showing the British public how well the troops were acclimatising to the not-so-harsh conditions of war. Second Ypres and the battles of 1916 soon put a stop to that.

The wood presented a swiftly-changing aspect as the seasons changed, with the bright colours of spring and summer superseding the dull damp ambience of winter, brightening up the spirits of the men that war had caused to live in it. Canon Scott, then the Padre to the 1st Canadian Division, was to remark that:

> The wood in those days was a very pleasant place to wander through. The little paths among the trees that whispered overhead in the summer breeze made one imagine that one was wandering through the forests of Canada.

Brigadier Croft, 9th (Scottish) Division, noted:

> When spring came what a perfect paradise it became with tender vistas of green everywhere.

This sense of euphoria seems to have deserted him as the weather warmed-up and visitors other than troops made their presence felt among the many damp and boggy sections of the wood. Just before the division left the Plugstreet Sector for its trek southward to the Somme battlefields, he mentioned curtly:

> Delighted now to leave Plugstreet Wood where the mosquitoes were beginning to make their presence felt!

Anthony Eden, apart from his opinion on the Hunter Avenue forts, also touches on the discipline expected of his 21st Battalion King's Royal Rifle Corps troops. During a meeting with his commanding officer, Lieutenant Colonel Lord Charles Duncombe, Earl of Feversham, he was to be reprimanded for his and his men's appearance. There had been heavy enemy shelling of the wood during the night and, in the early hours of the morning, men of his battalion were working hard at repairing the resulting gaps in their defences. The Earl Feversham, appearing later in the morning while the men were still hard at it, had said to Eden:

> You haven't shaved this morning, Anthony, nor have the men of your platoon.

Eden replied that he was well aware of this, but that he and his men had just experienced a bad night, to which Feversham had responded:

> I know, but you should all be shaved by nine. See to it next time.

Eden, rather crestfallen with his commanding officer's attitude, admits to being rather 'dunched', but had conceded that Lord Duncombe, although seemingly overly demanding in the circumstances, was quite correct.

'Duck Boards in Plug Street Wood' another C. M. Sheldon pencil drawing published in early 1918.

A series of sketches prepared by an anonymous artist
for publication in the *Illustrated London News*.

Plugstreet Hall

Somerset House

Scawby

Lord Charles Duncombe, Earl of Feversham, who had practically formed and brought the 21st Battalion from Yorkshire to the war at his own expense, would meet his death at the Hog's Head, Flers on 15 September 1916. He now lies buried in AIF Burial Ground, at Grass Lane, Flers in France.

Hunter Avenue would always be a place of sad memory for Anthony Eden. It was while the battalion was in reserve there just behind the wood's eastern edge where the reserve line trenches lay along Hunter Avenue that Eden lost his most capable non-commissioned officer and a very good friend, Sergeant Reg Park, during an enemy bombardment on 20 July 1916. He was killed by a direct hit on one of the small forts where he had been setting up rat traps in his efforts to suppress the invasion of an ever increasing number of these vermin which were taking toll of the battalion's rations as well as adding dirt and discomfort to an already dirty and uncomfortable environment. He was buried in the wood, but his grave was destroyed and lost in later shelling, as were many others. He is now remembered on the Ploegsteert Memorial to the Missing at Hyde Park Corner. A sergeant in the battalion in a letter to his mother wrote:

> This is what struck me as being very funny. You hear a Whiz! – Bang! – Cuckoo! The birds sing all the time the shells are bursting – it really is astonishing. The nightingales sing when the machine guns are firing during the night.

Once inside the silent grandeur of the wood, the soft breeze in the high branches makes it easy to imagine the bustle of activity, or the relaxing

British troops in 1914 on the pathway outside their log built cabins shelters inside the wood just south of Fosse Labarre, an old moat within the western side of the wood.

moments, created by those lords and masters of these glades who served here long ago – hundreds of them, resting, sleeping, strolling, singing, sky-larking, working away at their assigned duties or taking on the solemn task of burying a comrade, or tending the graves of those already at one with the earth.

The breeze conjures up this bustling activity, and the lazy inactivity, but it falls short of recalling the shouted instructions. the clattering noise of metal on metal, the crack of a rifle bullet, the drum roll of a machine-gun burst, the agonising screams of the wounded, the pitiful, whimpering calls of the scared, the slamming of guns, the snapping of branches at tree top level as shells and shrapnel forced their way through the growth, or the crashing of boughs finding their way to the woodland floor. Nor does it embrace the cold, wet, damp and dismal conditions caused by waterlogged ground that refused to drain.

The shallow trench lines and shell-holes that were once familiar surrounds are now almost levelled off, filled with fallen leaves and nature's compost, but they are there, as the unwary walker will find. Forts, once used to protect men from flying shards of metal, are now part-sunken concrete lumps, their sides, with the shapes of sandbags long since rotted away and their and earth covering long gone, stand in line alongside an overgrown Hunter Avenue. In other parts of the wood, similar relics, unnatural amongst the tall trees, the foliage and the wild flowers, stand, lonely and out of place. The dugouts and planked roads have gone, with not a trace of their being to mark the spots where men walked, worked and lived for their short term in this Belgian woodland.

More troops lingering at the corner where the pathway passing the log cabins intersected with a quiet and safe section of The Strand communication trench.

The three British military cemeteries in the wood, well kept and serene in their carefully tended enclaves, belie the clustering of the mounds of mud with wooden markers that once they were. To soldiers of the time, they represented fallen friends or comrades, or brought to mind the regiments who served

Peering over the breastwork on the edge of the wood.

Lighting up in the wood.

Breastworks in Bunhill Row.

here before them – making them constantly aware that, in the circumstances under which they were living, life was cheap. Today, they represent the fated men who were chosen to remain at war's end, acting as guardians of the inner-wood. The Toronto Avenue, Ploegsteert Wood and Rifle House military cemeteries are silent reminders to those who choose to walk within this woodland that many others were here for different reasons, and will still be there after the visitors have gone.

Life, for whatever garrison was in residency, was not always easy. Shelling apart, when it rained, conditions became very hard to bear. Slippery duck-boards, and the liquid mud soon turning into a quagmire, made passage for the multitude of carrying parties extremely tortuous. Men stumbled along the slip-pery boards and boggy tracks in the Flemish drizzle, struggling under heavy loads of rations and supplies upon which the men in the trench lines to the east depended. This was life on a daily basis during the less pleasant months of the year. Regiments were forever interchanging as the new formations moved into the wood and its trench lines to train and discover at first-hand what front-line life was really all about.

Although many were glad to see the back of this little woodland, a suffer-ing of a more intense kind awaited them further south on the uplands of the Somme and to the north in the infamous Ypres Salient itself. Many would have come to reflect in future months, if they were still around so to do, that their stint at Plugstreet had not really been that bad at all.

Hunter Avenue in 1918.

In direct contradiction to the sadness that surrounds the three military plots in the wood, and particularly that of Toronto Avenue, is the sight of the lush carpets of violets and cowslip that blanket this area of the wood in springtime.

Lieutenant Roland Leighton, 1/7th Battalion Worcestershire Regiment, 48th Division, while serving in the sector, had picked some of the violets that were growing on the top of his dugout to send to Vera Brittain his lover back in Britain. Vera Brittain, the mother of Shirley Williams, Member of Parliament, was to document their doomed romance in her book, *A Testament of Youth*.

On 25 April 1915, the day he sent the violets to Vera Brittain, Leighton had also sent to his mother a poem he had written about the violets in Plugstreet Wood:

Villanelle

Violets from Plug Street Wood,
Sweet, I send you oversea.
(It is strange they should be blue,
Blue, when his soaked blood was red,
For they grew around his head;
It is strange they should be blue.)

Violets from Plug Street Wood–
Think what they have meant to me–
Life and Hope and Love and You
(And you did not see them grow
Where his mangled body lay,
Hiding horror from the day;
Sweetest it was better so.)

Violets from oversea,
To you dear, far, forgetting land
These I send in memory,
Knowing You will understand.

Lieutenant Roland Leighton

Violets still in Plugstreet

How quiet the mystical wood appears at this time of day
The towering trees conspire in whispers, but in the softest way
Tranquil, is the perfect word to sum up this matchless mood
Can heaven's halls compare at all with this glorious interlude?

Tread softly stranger at the Toronto plot where Roland had his dreams
Did sunlit shafts in the sylvan wood remind him of gossamer beams?
Do you hear the echo of yesteryear as you pass Mud Corner by?
Did the boys, now dust beneath your feet, hear the winds wistful sigh?

As in a dream Roland picked the violets blue, all down Regent Street
A carpet blue that filled his soul, as he went forth to meet
The fate that had been ordained for him on another field of blood
And at Plugstreet Wood for evermore the violets blue will bud.

A tribute to Roland Leighton by Tony Spagnoly

Roland Leighton moved with the Worcesters to the Somme during late 1915 and, within six months of writing that memorable verse to his mother, he was lying in a soldier's grave at Louvencourt after being sniped whilst supervising a wiring party near Hébuterne just before the Christmas of that year.

Young men of Rifle House

The first strand of sunlight
bringing on the new day
filters through the wooded mass
to dapple on the rows of graves.
Breezes through the trees
create a dancing carousel upon the stones.
Diamonds of dew glisten on the grass around me
and the sweet caress of a bird's song
is the music of this wood.
Such beauty I cannot describe,
My only wish ...
to share it with those who lay here.
My eyes close
I sit, and think. And breath it all in
that feeling of peace and total calm ... a moment, then
a sense of guilt grips me
and shakes my thoughts.
How can I bask in this idyllic scene?
What these men went through
and now they are here,
what these men suffered
what these men saw.

How dare I ignore the meaning of this place,
my eyes close,
thoughts in turmoil
emotions struggling against themselves ... a moment, then
my eyes open and I can feel him there.
I cannot see him though I strain my eyes,
I can hear him but I cannot speak back.
He doesn't see the flowers
nor the brilliance of the place,
he just sees that I am there.
That is all they need.
What these men went through
so I could be there,
what these men went through
I remember, I care, ... a moment, then
I know he has gone
I am alone, but not quite,
I rise to leave
a last slow glance.,
Sleep well young men of Rifle House
you are in my heart forever.

Sue Brophy

In the Famous Plug Street Wood, an illustration by Fortunino Matania.

Regent Street today, reverting to its original quiet pathway on a southern fringe of the wood (Fortunino Matania can be forgiven in his use of poetic license in his impression of Regent Street as a pathway within the wood).

Songs from an Evil Wood

I.

There is no wrath in the stars,
  They do not rage in the sky;
I look from the evil wood
  And find myself wondering why.
Why do they not scream out
  And grapple star against star,
Seeking for blood in the wood,
  As all things round me are?
They do not glare like the sky
  Or flash like the deeps of the wood;
But they shine softly on
  In their sacred solitude.
To their happy haunts
  Silence from us has flown,
She whom we loved of old
  And know it now she is gone.
When will she come again
  Though for one second only?
She whom we loved is gone
  And the whole world is lonely.
And the elder giants come
  Sometimes, tramping from far,
Through the weird and flickering light
  Made by an earthly star.
And the giant with his club,
  And the dwarf with rage in his breath,
And the elder giants from far,
  They are the children of Death.
They are all abroad to-night
  And are breaking the hills with their brood,
And the birds are all asleep,
  Even in Plugstreet Wood.

II.

Somewhere lost in the haze
  The sun goes down in the cold,
And birds in this evil wood
  Chirrup home as of old;
Chirrup, stir and are still,
  On the high twigs frozen and thin.
There is no more noise of them now,
  And the long night sets in.
  Of all the wonderful things
That I have seen in the wood,
  I marvel most at the birds,
At their chirp and their quietude.
  For a giant smites with his club
All day the tops of the hill,
  Sometimes he rests at night,
Oftener he beats them still.
  And a dwarf with a grim black mane
Raps with repeated rage
  All night in the valley below
On the wooden walls of his cage.

III.

I met with Death in his country,
  With his scythe and his hollow eye
Walking the roads of Belgium.
  I looked and he passed me by.
Since he passed me by in Plug Street,
  In the wood of the evil name,
I shall not now lie with the heroes,
  I shall not share their fame;
I shall never be as they are,
  A name in the land of the Free,
Since I looked on Death in Flanders
  And he did not look at me.

Lord Dunsany

CHAPTER 6

GUARDIANS OF THE WOOD

A LTHOUGH NO MAJOR ACTIONS were to take place in the Plugstreet area from late 1914 until June 1917 casualties in this sector during the period were consistent, if low. Within the wood itself graves were gathered together in sections where early battalions had chosen to start regimental burial plots which were then used by later regiments serving in the area. Others were of nationalities other than that of the British casualties of the very early battles of the war. Some accounts talk of graves carrying simple crosses with inscriptions such as: "18 Soldiers of the 64th Saxon Regiment lie buried underneath." or: "Here lies a French Soldier", and often nothing gave a guide to those who lay under the many simple mounds dotted about the wood. Then there were those unfortunates who lay partially buried where they fell, covered only by a thin layer of slimy earth or part submerged in the stagnant content of a shell-hole. Often individual bodies would be buried in isolated spots, under a tree, in a small glade, or in a deserted part of the wood where they would be tended in private. Many of these individual graves were destroyed by later gunfire or, when the men who made them moved on, were neglected and lost forever. By all accounts though, most were diligently cared for, with damaged markers being frequently replaced and records of the graves being well kept. Many regimental histories and personal memoirs mention the well-tended graves within the wood and a particular account by Canon Scott, padre to the Canadian Divisions, is indicative of what must have been one of many similar occasions. One evening, when passing by a cemetery within the wood, he heard the sound of someone sobbing. He entered the plot and saw a young boy lying beside a newly-made grave. He attempted to console the boy who said to him:

It's the grave of my brother, Sir. He was buried this afternoon and now I have got to go back to the line without him.

How many men had to bear such grief, and with the knowledge that it could well be themselves lying in a grave in the not too distant future?

On the outer fringes of the wood, other regimental burial plots were begun and the many dressing stations in the area added their tally to the steady stream of casualties, all contributing to the massive task to be undertaken by the War

Graves Commission during the 1920s and 30s of collecting the dead for reburial in the official military cemeteries. After the gathering of the bodies and their concentration into their designated plots was eventually finalised, there began the more pleasant task of turning each cemetery into the red-bricked and white-stoned havens of rest as seen today.

There are over 450 of these military cemeteries in Belgium, with thirteen of them, together containing over 3,500 graves, forming a part-surround to the Plugstreet sector, excluding its eastern edge, the No-Man's Land and front line trenches of 1914-18. Their were originally nineteen cemeteries before the concentration of smaller burial plots and individual graves into the official military cemeteries implemented by the War Graves Commission. This number includes those of the Rozenberg Château and Rozenberg Château Extension that were removed from the château grounds in 1931 to become one cemetery just south of the Ploegsteert Memorial at Hyde Park Corner. This combination of plots is named as Berks Cemetery Extension (Rosenberg Château Plots)

The most northerly of these thirteen military cemeteries, sitting atop the rise overlooking the valley of the River Douve, is Prowse Point Military Cemetery. Started by the 2nd Battalion Royal Dublin Fusiliers and the 1st Battalion Royal Warwickshire Regiment, it was used from November 1914 to April 1918. It originally housed 214 war graves, 158 from the United Kingdom, 42 from New Zealand, 13 from Australia, one from Canada and 12 Germans who died as prisoners of war. These figures are now inaccurate as, in recent years it has been used as an 'open' cemetery with the remains of those found in the Plugstreet area being buried within.

On 3 January 2000 the remains of Private Harry Wilkinson, 2nd Battalion, Lancashire Fusiliers, 12th Brigade, 4th Division were discovered in a field just north of what used to be The Birdcage.

He had been killed in action on 10 November 1914 during an attack at Le Pelerin and was identified by his metal dog tag which had survived its many years beneath the earth. His burial was conducted by the Royal Regiment of Fusiliers in

Private Harry Wilkinson, 2nd Battalion, The Lancashire Fusiliers, who died 9 November 1914, and was buried in October 2000.

October 2001 with full military honours. Members of his family attended the ceremony as did the Duke of Kent, acting in his role as representative of the Commonwealth War Graves Commission of which he is President.

Harry Wilkinson's metal dog tag.

South of Prowse Point, down the slope along Mud Lane is Mud Corner British Cemetery, started at the outset of the Battle of Messines on 7 June 1917 by the New Zealanders and used until December of that year. It contains 85 graves, 53 from New Zealand, 31 from Australia and one from the United Kingdom. At this corner of Mud Lane is the only allowable and official entry to the wood wherein there are three cemeteries.

Mud Corner British Cemetery.

Soldiers graves alongside Mud Lane.

The first of these on the northern fringe of the wood, Toronto Avenue Cemetery, is one of the saddest cemeteries on the whole of the Western Front. Now at the end of a dark avenue of trees, it was named after a burial plot which was started close to the start of the Toronto Avenue communication trench running from just north of Moated Farm, parallel with the slope of Mud Lane. The lichen and moss from the trees here darken the stones, and all credit goes to the War Graves Commission gardeners for their constant, on-going efforts to maintain the cemetery to their usual high standards.

Although its name is obviously of Canadian origin, all 78 who lie here are men of the 9th Brigade, 3rd Australian Division who fell in the opening stages of the Battle of Messines between 7-10 June 1917. They fell just northeast of the wood near a well-fortified German stronghold called Grey Farm. Casualties mainly of the division's 33rd, 35th and 36th Battalions, most of them were hit by fire from a concealed machine-gun which caused havoc amongst the Australian attackers. They now rest together a world away from their homes, buried in a part of Belgian Flanders which they and their families possibly never knew existed. Each year on the Friday falling closest to 7 June, a memorial ceremony takes place in the cemetery attended by the Australian Ambassador to Belgium and local dignitaries.

Ploegsteert Wood Military Cemetery, the second cemetery of the three is, deeper in the wood and is made up of a number of small regimental plots totalling 163 graves covering the period 1914-17. Plot II was started by the 1st Battalion Somerset Light Infantry after the attack on The Birdcage in December

Toronto Avenue Cemetery.

South of Prowse Point, down the slope along Mud Lane is Mud Corner British Cemetery, started at the outset of the Battle of Messines on 7 June 1917 by the New Zealanders and used until December of that year. It contains 85 graves, 53 from New Zealand, 31 from Australia and one from the United Kingdom. At this corner of Mud Lane is the only allowable and official entry to the wood wherein there are three cemeteries.

Mud Corner British Cemetery.

Soldiers graves alongside Mud Lane.

The first of these on the northern fringe of the wood, Toronto Avenue Cemetery, is one of the saddest cemeteries on the whole of the Western Front. Now at the end of a dark avenue of trees, it was named after a burial plot which was started close to the start of the Toronto Avenue communication trench running from just north of Moated Farm, parallel with the slope of Mud Lane. The lichen and moss from the trees here darken the stones, and all credit goes to the War Graves Commission gardeners for their constant, on-going efforts to maintain the cemetery to their usual high standards.

Although its name is obviously of Canadian origin, all 78 who lie here are men of the 9th Brigade, 3rd Australian Division who fell in the opening stages of the Battle of Messines between 7-10 June 1917. They fell just northeast of the wood near a well-fortified German stronghold called Grey Farm. Casualties mainly of the division's 33rd, 35th and 36th Battalions, most of them were hit by fire from a concealed machine-gun which caused havoc amongst the Australian attackers. They now rest together a world away from their homes, buried in a part of Belgian Flanders which they and their families possibly never knew existed. Each year on the Friday falling closest to 7 June, a memorial ceremony takes place in the cemetery attended by the Australian Ambassador to Belgium and local dignitaries.

Ploegsteert Wood Military Cemetery, the second cemetery of the three is, deeper in the wood and is made up of a number of small regimental plots totalling 163 graves covering the period 1914-17. Plot II was started by the 1st Battalion Somerset Light Infantry after the attack on The Birdcage in December

Toronto Avenue Cemetery.

1914. It holds 32 graves of men of the regiment and 10 of their colleagues are at rest in Plot I. The cemetery embraces the graves of 118 from the United Kingdom, 28 from Canada, 18 from New Zealand, one from Australia and one unidentified.

Rifle House Cemetery is the third in the wood and, with its tall tree-surround in stark contrast to Toronto Avenue, is one of the loveliest in Belgium. 230 British and one Canadian rest here. The reason for the lone

The officer's section of the 1st Battalion Somerset Light Infantry plot in Ploegsteert Wood Military Cemetery, December 1914. These five officers died in the raid on German House on 19 Dec. 1914 (See page 27).

Ploegsteert Wood Military Cemetery today.

Canadian grave will remain one of those mysteries that so often accompany burials along the whole length of the Western Front. Many graves are of those who fell during The Birdcage attack on 19 December 1914. Young Rifleman Barnett is here, together with Captain the Honourable Morgan-Grenville, his company commander, and Captain the Honourable Prittie the second-in-command of the 1st Battalion Rifle Brigade involved in that raid. Rifle House Cemetery was begun in November 1914 and takes its name from the log hut headquarters which existed close by.

Below the wood on the Plugstreet-Warneton road is Lancashire Cottage Cemetery. Started by the 1st East Lancs (84 graves) and the 1st Hampshires (56

Wooden crosses in Rifle House Cemetery marking the graves of the Hons. R. G. Morgan Grenville and F. R. D. Prittie who died in the raid on German House on 19 Dec. 1914 (See page 26).

Rifle House Cemetery today.

THE GUARDIANS

here, Second Lieutenant Richard John Lumley, a young cavalryman from Belgravia, London, killed in action on 17 October 1914 is one of the earliest casualties to be found in the Ypres Salient, being buried even before the 'race to the sea' ended. Two at rest here served with the 7th Battalion (British Columbia) Canadian Expeditionary Force, part of the 1st Canadian Division, some of the earliest casualties suffered by this division as it moved to the sector in the winter of 1915. Laid out in one single line of headstones, the cemetery contains nine graves: seven from the United Kingdom (six from the 1st Battalion, Hampshire Regiment) and two from Canada.

North of the village on the right side of the road is an area housing The Australian Central Dressing Station named Charing Cross. This area gave access to The Strand communication trench, a major route for troops moving eastward through the wood to the trenches. Today, this clearing is the site of Strand Military Cemetery. Two burials were made here in October 1914 and it wasn't used again until April 1917 when 351 graves were completed, 232 of which are Australian. Housing casualties of the Messines offensive in June of that year, the cemetery was known as the Australian Cemetery, only acquiring its current title after the concentration of graves into one cemetery by the War Graves Commission during the 1920s. Seven hundred and seventy-seven graves were collected from small cemeteries between Wytschaete and Armentières and from behind the German lines to complete today's cemetery. It now contains the graves and memorials of 1,148 men, 725 soldiers and one airman from the United Kingdom, 285 from Australia, 87 from New Zealand, 26 from Canada, one from South Africa and four of German prisoners. Unnamed British graves total 356 with 13 United Kingdom soldiers, five Australians and one New Zealander having special memorials. One of these, that of Lance Corporal

Ploegsteert Churchyard Military Cemetery, nine graves laid out in a single line in the Plugstreet village churchyard.

Herbert Prior, 34th Battalion, Australian Imperial Force was commemorated on 7 June 2002 after research determined he was 'Believed to be buried in the cemetery' as the inscription on the headstone indicates. He had been killed in the Australian rest dugouts in nearby Bunhill Row on 10 June 1917 during an enemy bombardment. His battalion had just come out of the line following their involvement in the opening stages of the Battle of Messines. He had been taken to the Charing Cross Dressing Station plot and buried, but his grave was lost during later bombardments of the area. The Charing Cross Dressing Station itself is still in place today, but is now used as a part aviary and part tool shed

The Australian Cemetery as it was before the War Graves Commission's concentration of graves caused it to be Plots I–VI in the Strand Military Cemetery. The house to the left was rebuilt on it's original site.

The Australian Cemetery Plots I–VI in today's cemetery

Lance Corporal Herbert Prior, 34th Battalion, A.I.F.

by the farmer on whose land it stands.

Two of the unnamed are unidentified RAF graves of July 1918, originally buried in the Le Touquet Berthe Farm German cemetery. Eight graves in this cemetery are of men who died in the Second World War when British units garrisoned the area in 1940 prior to the Dunkirk evacuation.

Further north on the left side of the road to Messines at Hyde Park Corner is a grouping of two cemeteries and a memorial. Normally taken to be one cemetery they in fact represent a memorial and two extensions of the original cemetery across the road just below Mud Lane. The first, Berks Cemetery Extension

Lance Corporal H Prior's special memorial headstone at Strand Military Cemetery.

The Strand Military Cemetery concentration of graves with the original plots to the right of the rebuilt house pictured at the rear of the cemetery.

The Ploegsteert Memorial at Hyde Park Corner, with the Berks Cemetery Extension (Rosenberg Château Plots) in the foreground.

(Rosenberg Château Plots) contains the graves of 477 men, of which 171 are from the United Kingdom, 145 from Canada, 126 from Australia and 35 from New Zealand, all originally buried near the Rosenberg Château Dressing Station at the base of the southern slope of Hill 63 in a cemetery started in November 1914 by units of the United Kingdom. In May 1916, an extension was started and used mainly by Australian and New Zealand units during the build up to the Messines Offensive in 1917. After the war, the owner of the château refused to allow the cemeteries to rest on his land and in 1931 each soldier was exhumed and, with full military honours, made his short, final journey to the bottom of Hill 63 and reburied in this extension.

The Berks Cemetery Extension in the 1920s

Berks Cemetery Extension in 2003

Just north of the Rosenberg Château plots is the imposing Ploegsteert Memorial. Designed by Mr. H. Charlton Bradshaw, the Memorial was inaugurated by the Belgian Prince, the Duke of Brabant, on 7 June 1931. There being no local airfield, the Duke of Brabant had flown directly to Courtrai, from where he was driven to the village square. A procession was formed and made its way along the Messines–Armentières road to the memorial site. After its unveiling, massed bands accompanied by choirs of schoolchildren, played both the Belgian and the British national anthems. The memorial commemorates 11,447 men who have no known graves and who fell in the Battles of Armentières, Aubers Ridge, Loos, Fromelles, Estaires, Hazebrouck, Scherpenberg and Outtersterne Ridge. Sergeant Reginald Park, 21st Battalion, King's Royal Rifle Corps, whose death was detailed by Sir Anthony Eden, is remembered here and four Victoria Cross holders are featured on its panels: Sapper W. Hackett VC, 254th Company, Royal Engineers, killed in action 27 June 1916; Captain W. H. Johnstone VC, 59th Company, Royal Engineers, killed in action 8 June 1915; Private J. Mackenzie VC, 2nd Scots Guards, killed in action 19 December 1914; and Acting Captain T. P. Pryce VC, 4th Grenadier Guards, killed in action 13 April 1918.

In recent years a memorial committee formed by the local Ploegsteert community has organised the sounding of Last Post at 7 pm on the first Friday of each month in remembrance and as a tribute to the British dead who fell in the Great War.

Just north of the memorial, is the Berks Cemetery Extension. Originally sited on the other side of the road, it was started in June 1916 and used until September 1917. It holds the graves of 394 of the fallen, 295 from the United Kingdom, 51 from Australia, 45 from New Zealand and three from Canada. The

Hyde Park Corner (Royal Berks) Cemetery.

cemetery to which this was an extension is situated on the opposite side of the road, facing Hyde Park Corner. Called Hyde Park Corner (Royal Berks) Cemetery, it was started by the 1/4th Battalion Royal Berkshire Regiment in the spring of 1915 and used until November 1917. Amongst the gathering of 87 graves is that of 16-year-old Rifleman Albert French, 18th Battalion, King's Royal Rifle Corps to whom this book is dedicated. Also buried here is Private F. Giles, 1/4th Battalion Royal Berkshire Regiment, the first fatality of the regiment while serving in the wood and Lieutenant Ronald Poulton Palmer, also of the 1/4th Royal Berks, the regiment's first officer casualty, killed by a sniper on the morning of 5 May 1915. Four Germans who died in captivity are buried here, as are some of those who died without honour having been sentenced to death by court martial. Of the 87 graves, 81 are from the United Kingdom, one from Canada, one from Australia and four of German prisoners.

Opposite this cemetery Red Lodge Road, branching off the Messines–Armentières road at Hyde Park Corner, makes its way to Romarin, passing the southerly entrances to The Catacombs and Red Lodge house at the Rosenberg Château driveway, before turning sharply left where, on its right is Underhill Farm. To the left of the farm, sits Underhill Farm Cemetery. Started in June 1917 for the New Zealand Division's Messines offensive Central Dressing Station sited in the farm, it holds casualties from the Battle of Messines and was used until January 1918 when it fell into German hands. One hundred and ninety-one graves are here, 103 from the United Kingdom, 47 from Australia, 39 from New Zealand one from Canada and one whose unit is unknown.

These thirteen cemeteries in and around Plugstreet Wood reflect the care and effort made by the Commonwealth War Graves Commission in maintaining British military cemeteries throughout the world.

Underhill Farm Cemetery alongside Underhill Farm with Red Lodge in the far distance.

CHAPTER 7

SHOW-PIECE OF THE WESTERN FRONT

T HE OCTOBER TO DECEMBER PERIOD OF 1914 is often ignored when writing about the Plugstreet sector. Not many of the Old Contemptibles and the early territorial units considered it worth writing about as to them, war was war and they just got on with the job of waging it. Many regimental histories feature accounts of the area which defy understanding when compared with one another:

... For hours on end men had to stand in trenches, often three feet deep in water, with gale and wind blowing and in driving rain, wet to the skin, shivering and shaking from cold and worn with fatigue

... they stood in water, with walls of oozy mud about them, until their legs rotted and became black with a false frost-bite, until many of them were carried away with bronchitis and pneumonia, and until all of them, however many body-belts they used, were shivering sodden, scarecrows plastered with mud, and they crawled with lice.

Compared with:

...In the war on the Western Front, 'Plug Street' will always be connected with peace. This sector represented the nursery to which many divisions were sent on their first arrival in France, and a haven of rest to tired divisions, both of ourselves and the enemy.

It is hard to believe that the accounts refer to the same place.

A 'cushy' posting it undoubtedly was when compared with other parts of the Ypres Salient, and the wood is often mentioned as a pleasant place to have been. Criss-crossed with rides and fire alleys, men listened to the singing of nightingales and admired the wild flowers and lush foliage while undergoing instruction which would serve them well in other parts of the front line. Lieutenant Ronald Poulton Palmer, 1/4th Royal Berkshires wrote to his family:

... It is a beautiful walk to the farm where the headquarters are, through the wood blooming with cowslips and bluebells, past two or three beautifully kept graves.

Captain C.R.M.F. Cruttwell of the same regiment was clearly enchanted:

... in the spring and summer of 1915 it was a beautiful place, where one might fancy the many British dead rested more easily beneath oaks and among familiar flowers than in most of the cemeteries in this dreary land ... its undergrowth when not cut away, was densely intertwined with alder, hazel, ash and blackthorn, with water standing in large pools on parts of its boggy surface ... everywhere the dog violet and blue veronica flourished in enormous clumps, and near The Strand was a great patch of Solomon's seal.

That it was 'idyllic' to serve in the wood is obviously an exaggeration, but many of the men who served there do recall their time with similar descriptions.

German infantry advancing through the wood in their 1918 spring offensive.

Charing Cross, the Australian Advanced Dressing Station, today.

Then there is the other side of the story. Aubrey Smith in his classic *Four Years on the Western Front* notes:

There had been so much fighting in this wood that there were hundreds of dead bodies in it and the streams are somewhat polluted with them. The most smells come from behind the lines, where there were many bodies lying around.

The Somerset Light Infantry history recalls:

The rides through the wood, the only possible way back to the support trenches, were three-feet deep in mud, through which men floundered and struggled in the darkness to reach their destination.

Sergeant Arthur Cook of the 1st Battalion of that regiment wrote:

Another day of hell under the continual hail of shells and bullets ... men are being buried alive and blown to pieces all around me. Perhaps death is preferable to this infernal life.

The 36th (Ulster) Divisional history states:

... sown with wire 'Plug Street Wood' being such a tangle that it has always been a mystery to those who saw it how the Germans passed through it in 1918

The Indian Corps noted:

... a sparsely-treed patch nearly three-miles long by three-quarters of a mile wide. The ground was mostly bog, while the slightest rain rendered the road almost impassable.

The Canadians and New Zealanders write of the particular efficiency of the German snipers who seemed to have covered the wood and its occupants from

Men of the 6th Siege Battery RFA drawing rations at Underhill Farm in 1914

every conceivable angle, making any movement along the eastern areas of the wood's interior extremely hazardous to life.

The Australians, moving to their positions at the opening of the Messines Offensive in 1917, had to traverse the wood in which gas lay in the dense air. It was under heavy German bombardment and the track taken by some through Bunhill Row and Mud Lane was strewn with officers and men who had collapsed under a combination of effort and gas inhalation. The rush of casualties, combined with difficult working conditions, caused the medics at

A Labour Company site during the clearing-up operations at Plugstreet after the Armistice.

The grass-covered footings of Château de la Hutte.

the Australian Charing Cross Central Dressing Station, themselves wearing gas masks, to divert a great number of their cases to the New Zealand Dressing Station at Underhill Farm. So much for the tranquillity of the wood.

After the battles of 1914 and early 1915 when the trench lines had formed a deadlock along the whole of the Western Front, the Plugstreet Sector did become a reasonably safe spot to serve, in as much as any front-line sector in wartime can be a safe spot to serve. Eventually it, and Plugstreet Wood in particular, became the army's show-piece where journalists, politicians and other distinguished visitors could be escorted to the Tourist Line, a reserve line of breastworks in front of Hunter Avenue, to gain 'first-hand experience' of what it was like to be 'at the front'. The ten generals at the opening of The Catacombs, Churchill's exploit in the trench lines at Le Gheer with his dinner-guests and the use of the Tourist Line, and all that its name implies, bear evidence to the fact that Plugstreet was considered a fairly safe area

Although a sector that experienced nothing like the raging battles of other parts of the Western Front, it held much meaning for the individual soldier who served there. In the post-war years, as with all areas of this war-torn country, farms were rebuilt, roads relaid and the many scattered burial plots brought together to take their place in the network of military cemeteries spanning the old Western Front. Nevertheless, many traces of the war still scar the area around Plugstreet and bring to mind events of the past – the shell-battered ground embracing the grass-covered footings and cellars of Château de la Hutte; the lodge at the entrance to the old grounds of Rosenberg Château and the corner of the road fork below the original site of the château that marks the first burial plots of the bodies of those men who were exhumed and now rest in the Berks Cemetery Extension (Rosenberg Château Plots) at Hyde Park

Mule and motor transport at Hyde Park Corner in October 1915.

Corner. Hyde Park Corner itself, no longer a crossroads but still a place to prompt thought and to conjure-up visions of constant traffic moving up and down Red Lodge Road servicing the many camps, stores, dumps and mustering points sited along its length to Romarin; the entrances to The Catacombs, an engineering feat for which the Australians deserve great credit; the sentry hut in the forecourt of The Piggeries, the water-filled mine craters where stood the German strongpoints obliterated at the beginning of the Battle of Messines, and many, many more. Plugstreet Wood itself has been heavily cut back since the

The sentry box in the forecourt of The Piggeries.

The 'report centre' at one of the three southerly entrance/exits to The Catacombs at Hill 63.

Great War but many of the rides and fire alleys in the wood still traverse it, although no longer marked with their distinctive street names. The ground still resembles a boggy morass when the rains come. The seven small forts remain to line Hunter Avenue, the Blighty Hall dressing station still stands to mark the spot where so much work of the 'medics' was carried out; these being just eight of the thirty two known concrete structures that are dotted about within the wood. Half sunken, mostly filled with water, odd shaped and ugly, they bear witness to the times when they were put to use, whatever that was. The

The Factory Farm water-filled mine crater edged with trees as it is today.

The sister to the Factory Farm crater in 2003, named Ultimo Crater due to its position at the southern start to the German Ultimo trench.

One of the small forts along Hunter Avenue mentioned in Anthony Eden's *Another World*.

A shelter or command centre built by New Zealand engineers for the Battle of Messines.

Partly destroyed shelter.

Another shelter, well below ground.

Large shelter, command post or HQ structure.

reason for the being of some are obvious, for others, not so. Nevertheless they sit squat and alone as they have done since the war years, reminding those who manage to see them that the wood was an integral part of the conflict that embraced this sector of what was once the Western Front. Nevertheless, the cowslips, violets and bluebells still bloom in profusion and, above them, the nightingales still sing.

In the post-war years this show-piece of the old Western Front continued to attract visitors, distinguished and otherwise, and it still does! Nowadays, the

The Blighty Hall Dressing Station.

Another subterranean shelter.

Plugstreet Wood. A watercolour by F E Hodge RFA.

roads and accommodation are better, and there's nobody around ready to take a pot-shot at them, unless of course they enter the main body of the wood without permission and a gamekeeper decides to take decisive action in protecting his game birds. Nevertheless, Plugstreet and its' woodland does not always feature as a priority on the battlefield visitor's list of places to visit when in the Ypres sector. Many hurry past its leafy mass in coaches or personal vehicles with hardly a second glance as the Somme and points south beckon, but for those who do visit nowadays, the best time is down to the circumstances and desire of the individual.

A well-constructed firing post.

A channel leading into a sunken concrete reservoir.

Advanced Estaminet, Warneton, Belgium on the corner where the Anton's Farm road meets the Messines–Armentières road – A watercolour by Lawrence Preston.

The house on the corner where once stood Advanced Estaminet.

A 'rewarding' experience is being there on a cold, damp, drizzling, miserable winter evening as darkness, deep impenetrable darkness, cloaks the wood and its environs, walking in whatever direction takes the fancy, sensing the menace of The Birdcage, and being aware of the men who died attacking it, now resting, since 1914, deep within the wood. A visit to the graves in their

The entrance to the Strand running alongside today's Strand Military Cemetery.

The house now standing on the site of Bruce Bairnsfather's cottage.

Rotten Row running down to the wood from Bruce Bairnsfather's cottage.

orderly ranks arouses deep sentiments and following the walks of Bruce Bairnsfather when checking his outlying machine-gun posts digs deep into the reserves of stamina and persistence. Walking by the turnip field just north of St. Yves, imagining the scene of the gathering of men of both armies during the truce of Christmas 1914 gives much food for thought and scrambling down the slippery, muddy slope of Rotten Row by Bairnsfather's cottage site or, better still, down Mud Lane, past Moated Farm, entering the wood at Mud Corner and trudging to the old Tourist Line, brings to mind the Royal Scots resisting an enemy raid, and of the fearful eruptions just across the way at Factory Farm

Mud Lane at its original meeting point with the Messines–Armentières road just after the war, no longer "strewn with officers and men". The clump of 'trees' in the background-centre was the "verdant thicket of little willows and blackberry bushes" where Talbot Kelly's section had a forward gun.

Mud Lane where it meets the Messines–Armentières road today. It originally cut through the small section of ploughed land to the right joining the road at Hyde Park Corner. The clump of trees in the centre was Talbot Kelly's "verdant thicket".

and Ultimo craters. Stumbling along to Blighty Hall then back up Fleet Street, turning left into the The Strand, by-passing the cemetery named after it to take a look in the gloomy darkness at the three-chambered Charing Cross dressing station that saw much Australian suffering in 1917, then back down the Messines–Armentières road to the Plugstreet village square is difficult enough, but its a lot easier than taking a similar trip when wet and cold, stumbling and staggering whilst gripping one end of a stretcher. Taking the long walk from Plugstreet village to Le Gheer crossroads, pausing a while at the ditch where the Germans set up their defences after pushing back the Inniskillings, is

Hants Farm on its original site, and still partly surrounded my its moat, but no longer a collecting point for materials and water supplies by troop carrying parties.

Hull's Burnt Farm now sited to the left of its original position. The clump of trees to its right mark what is left of the moat which once surrounded the farm.

demanding, passing the site of Keeper's Hut between the crossroads and Hunter Avenue prompts thoughts of the squat 'forts' running alongside the 'Avenue', but standing at the crossroads facing the old No-Man's Land is an experience unto itself. By staying there long enough, and with the imagination running free, sights and sounds of the Somersets clearing the little houses at the point of the bayonet, or the burial parties laying their men to rest in the fields opposite over the Christmas 1914 period, British and German alike, come

A tranquil Touquet Berthe Farm, no longer a military supply dumping area ...

... and a Moated Farm (now a private residence) nestling on the edge of a quiet wood.

to the receptive mind with an ease that is disturbing. The possibilities are endless, the thoughts brought to mind boundless.

Feeling the damp, the cold and the weariness prompts thoughts toward a nice warm fire, a soft bed and the comfort of knowing that walking the battle-areas can be enjoyable, and particularly so without cloying, mud-filled tracks to stumble along, or the burden of rain-soaked khaki-coloured serge clothing, mud-heavy boots, rifle, ammunition, wooden planks, bales of empty sandbags, ration sacks, water tins, rolls of wire or whatever else High Command had deemed should be carried by men in wartime – and, of course, without the crump of the odd shell, or the burst of machine-gun fire, the echoing crack of a rifle shot or the buzz of a passing bullet to liven up the otherwise pleasant silence of the night.

The visitor could then do it all again in much more pleasant, comfortable and enjoyable conditions, early on a bright spring morning, or even a tranquil autumn evening, and then once again on a balmy summer's day when the buzzing will be the noise of industrious bees.

The discomforts will be replaced by all the nicer things that attend such leisurely times, and enjoying them need not be overshadowed by the thought that many alert, highly-trained military men, wearing the uniform coloured field grey are in position to the north and east of the wood. Their sole reason for being there? To detect and identify whatever movement they can, and to violently eliminate its cause.

That was for those who walked this way in years past.

A view of Plugstreet Wood from Mud Lane looking down Bunhill Row, now devoid of its planked road, rest camps and breastworks.

Nevertheless visitor, give it some thought, let the imagination run free, go back to Prowse Point, then down Mud Lane, passing Mud Corner Cemetery on into the wood, wander again Toronto Avenue, Ploegsteert Wood and Rifle House cemeteries within the wood, make your way, to Lancashire Cottage Cemetery and then the three grouped around the Plugstreet Memorial. Reflect awhile ... think deep. You will not have experienced what those men who lie at rest did, but you will have trod a little way in their footsteps. Then you can say that you have felt just some of what this show-piece called Plugstreet Wood has to offer - and you will surely come again.

A quieter, safer, but much overgrown Hunter Avenue still traverses the wood from south to north.

BIBLIOGRAPHY

10th Battalion Argyll and Sutherland Highlanders, 1914-1919.
Lieutenant-Colonel Herbert G. Sotheby, D.S.O., M.V.O.
John Murray, London, 1931.

48th Highlanders of Canada 1891-1928.
Kim Beattie. 48th Highlanders of Canada, 1932.

A Soldier's War. Arthur Henry Cook, D.C.M., M.M., B.E.M. and Lieutenant-General G.N. Molesworth, C.S.I., O.B.E. E.Goodman & Sons. Ltd., Taunton.

A Subaltern's Odyssey. R. B. Talbot Kelly. William Kimber & Co. Ltd., 1980.

A Territorial Soldier's War. Bryan Latham. Gale & Polden Ltd., 1967.

Another World 1897 - 1917. Anthony Eden. Allen Lane, 1976.

Amid the Guns Below. The Story of the Canadian Corps, 1914-1919.
Larry Worthington. McClelland & Stewart Ltd., Toronto, 1965.

Bairnsfather, A Few Fragments from His Life.
Collected by a friend. The Bystander, Hodder & Stoughton.

Bullets & Billets. Bruce Bairnsfather. Grant Richards Ltd., London, 1916.

Testament of Youth. Vera Brittain. Victor Gollancz Ltd., London, 1935.

Courage Remembered. Edwin Gibson and Kingsley Ward, H.M.S.O., 1989.

Drummer Spencer John Bent, V.C.
H.L. Kirby and R.R. Walsh. T.H.C.L. Books, Blackburn, 1986.

Four Years on the Western Front. By a Rifleman. Odhams Press, 1922.

Gentlemen and Officers. K.W. Mitchinson. Imperial War Museum, 1995.

History of the East Lancashire Regiment in the Great War 1914 - 1918.
Littlebury Bros. Ltd.., Liverpool, 1936.

In Search of the Better 'Ole.
Tonie and Valmai Holt. Milestone Publications, 1985.

My Sapper Venture. Lieutenant-Colonel V.F. Eberle, M.C.
Pitman Publishing, 1973.

Rifle Brigade Chronicles 1914 and 1916. Colonel Willoughby Verner.
John Bale, Sons & Danielsson Ltd., London, 1915 and 1917.

Salient Points. Tony Spagnoly and Ted Smith. Pen & Sword Ltd., 1995.

The 13th Battalion Royal Highlanders of Canada 1914 - 1919.
R.C. Fetherstonhaugh. 13th Battalion, Royal Highlanders of Canada, 1925.

The Blazing Trail of Flanders. T Lloyd. Heath Cranton Ltd., London, 1933.

The First Buckinghamshire Battalions 1914 - 1919.
Captain P.L. Wright, D.S.O., M.C. Hazell, Watson & Viney, Ltd., 1920.

The Great War as I saw it. Canon Frederick George Scott, C.M.G., D.S.O.
The Clarke & Stuart Co. Ltd. 1934.

The History of the 9th (Scottish) Division.
John Ewing M.C., John Murray, London, 1921.

The History of the 11th (Lewisham) Battalion The Queen's Own Royal West Kent Regiment.
Capt. R.O. Russell, M.C. Lewisham Newspaper Co. Ltd., London, 1934.

The History of the London Rifle Brigade 1859 - 1919.
Constable & Co. Ltd., 1921.

The History of the Rifle Brigade in the War of 1914 - 1918. Vol. I, August 1914 - December 1916.
Reginald Berkeley, M.C. The Rifle Brigade Club Ltd., 1927.

The History of the Somerset Light Infantry (Prince Albert's) 1914 - 1919.
Everard Wyrall. Methuen & Co. Ltd., 1927.

The Life of Ronald Poulton.
Edward Bagnall Poulton. Sidgwick & Jackson, 1919.

The Official History of Australia the War of 1914-18, volume IV,
The A.I.F. in France. Dr. C.E.W. Bean. Angus and Robertson Ltd.,
Sidney, Australia, 1933

The Official History of New Zealand's Effort in the Great War, Vol II, France.
Colonel H. Stewart. C.M.G.,D.S.O.,M.C. Whitcomb and Tombs Ltd.,
New Zealand, 1921.

The Official History of the War, Military Operations, 1914-1918,
France and Belgium 1914, Volume II.
Brigadier-General J.E. Edmonds. MacMillan and Co. Ltd., 1915.

The Royal Berkshire Regiment Vol II, 1914 - 1918.
F. Loraine Petre, O.B.E. The Barracks, Reading, 1925.

The Royal Scots 1914 - 1919, Vol. I.
Major John Ewing, M.C. Oliver & Boyd, 1925.

The Royal Inniskillings Fusiliers in the Great War.
Sir Frank Fox, O.B.E. Constable & Company Ltd., 1928.

The Story of the 2/5th Battalion Gloucestershire Regiment 1914 - 1918.
A. F. Barnes, M.C. The Crypt House Press Ltd., 1930.

The V.C. and D.S.O. Sir O'Moore Creagh, V.C., G.C.B., G.C.S.I. and
E.M. Humphris. The Standard Art Book Co. Ltd., London, 1924.

The War Story of the 1/4 Royal Berkshire Regiment (T.F.).
C.R.M.F. Cruttwell. Oxford Basil Blackwell, 1922.

The Ypres Times. Ford & Gill, London, January 1928 – July 1935.

Thoughts and Adventures. The Right Honourable Winston S. Churchill,
C.H., M.P. Thornton Butterworth, Ltd., London, 1932.

Three years with the 9th Division.
Lieutenant-Colonel W.D. Croft, C.M.G., D.S.O. John Murray, London. 1919.

Tunnellers. Captain W. Grant Grieve and Bernard Newman.
Herbert Jenkins Ltd., London. 1936.

War Underground. Alexander Barrie. Frederick Muller Ltd. London. 1962.

With the Indians in France.
General Sir James Willcocks G.C.M.G., K.C.B., K.C.S.I., D.S.O., LL.D.
Constable and Co. Ltd. London, 1920.

With Winston Churchill at the Front.
Captain X, Gowans & Gray, Ltd., London, 1924.

Your Loving Brother Albert. The letters of Albert French boy soldier 1915 -1916.
The Estate of Albert French. The People's Press of Milton Keynes, 1983.

Private papers. Tom Gudmestad, Seattle, U.S.A.

Private papers. Tony Spagnoly, London.

Private papers. Ted Smith, London.

INDEX

Cemeteries & Memorials